A WOMAN'S GUIDE TO CHOOSING HER BREED OF MAN

MEN ARE DOGS

— JEANNETTE WRIGHT —

Illustrator Mike McCartney

BROWN BOOKS PUBLISHING GROUP
DALLAS, TEXAS

Illustrations by Mike McCartney

Cover photo by John Pingenot

Cover models: Joel Silvey, and Trinity, the Jack Russell Terrier from Sunset Acres Jack Russell Terriers

For information, please contact Brown Books Publishing Group
16200 North Dallas Parkway,
Suite 170, Dallas, Texas 75248
www.brownbooks.com
972-381-0009

ISBN 0-9743068-0-0
LCCN 2003111338

First Printing, 2003

MEN ARE DOGS

Bow Wow,

James Wight

Dedication

Dedicated to all breeds of men and dogs,
including the mutts.
May they find happy homes
and appreciation for who they are.
And to

Blanca
MAY 1989 – JULY 2003

Contents

Acknowledgments

A HEART-WARM thank you and many hugs to: Cathy Carrington, Sherri Galaway, Krystyna Jurzykowski, Mary Anne Redmond, Barbara Whiddon, and Maria Whitworth, who supported me in numerous ways; my favorite dog illustrator, Mike McCartney; Brown Books Publishing Group who brought excellence to the book; my brother John Pingenot for the photos; my parents, Jean and Duwain Pingenot, for encouraging me throughout all my endeavors; Jan Kirshner, who gave the book heart when I wasn't sure what it needed; story contributors Cindy Albury and Jon Conrad, Victoria and Jerry Ayers, Donna Collins and Bruce Yamani, Ray Gin, Rod and Isabella Russell-Ides, Yvonne Klusman and Erich Geissler, Charise and Bryan Moses, Jimmy Lynn Moses, Linda and Kent Savage, Jim Stone, Lisa and Ted Vann, Barbara and Michael Whiddon, Julie and Steve Wilke, Bonnie Wright, La Nell Wright, Ray Wright and more; models for the cover, Joel Silvey, and Trinity the Jack Russell Terrier, from Sunset Acres Jack Russell Terriers.

A big "thanks" goes to certain people who made a difference whether or not they were aware of it. This includes Michael Stern, Tom Elliot, Flicker Hammond, Charles Richards, Donald Epstein and Jackie Knowles,

Brian Moreland, Tyree Beaton, Lindell Lewis, Sherri, Ted, and Jasmine Eck, and all my nieces and nephews—Josh, Ryan, Luke, Fletcher, Tanner, Heather, Shannon, and Maycee. I wish to thank all the men, be they acquaintances, friends, relatives, or boyfriends, who have been in my life. It is because of them that I can appreciate men and have fun writing this book.

For all the dogs in my life and the invaluable lessons they taught me, especially Shaka and Strider, who kept me company while I wrote. And while they may not be the subject of the book, my cats, Blanca and Sheer Khan, who slept near me (or on my papers) during much of the writing. And, finally, my biggest thanks go to my husband, Lance Wright, the Borzoi who believed in me and this project during all its phases. He makes my life better by being in it!

Introduction

IMAGINE, FOR a moment, that men are like dogs. You may have noticed this. They may mess up your house, bark at you to get their way, and sometimes run off to another woman. But there is a bright side to these lovable canines. Since men are like dogs, they're not that complicated. If you feed them, pet them, praise them, respect them, and let them do the things they're good at, they're usually content and will be loyal, devoted, and loving partners. It may sound simple, but if that's all it takes . . .

Why is the divorce rate so high? Why do so many relationships fail? People may say it was just a bad relationship or he was a bad man, but there are very few bad relationships or bad men. For women, it is more empowering to take responsibility for our choices. The reason many relationships fail is that many of us pick the wrong breed of man.

"Dogs are not our whole life, but they make our lives whole."
ROGER CARAS

Let's say a woman, Ann, wants a man who will wait on her hand and foot. She wants him to have a successful career so that she can quit her job and have children. She would like him to be easy to train. If she asks him to mow the lawn, it's done. Then one day she meets John, who, is playful, sweet, and makes her feel special. And because he makes her feel special, she falls in love and creates a story about their future life. John doesn't talk much about his job and likes to lie around and watch TV for hours, but Ann thinks his habits will change once they're married. Unfortunately for Ann, she's picked a Pug, and Pugs are lap men who love to be pampered and prefer not to work. Of course they're fun and playful, which is why Ann was initially attracted to John. But the ideal breed for Ann is the Golden Retriever which will work hard to provide for her and lovingly be there for her. And, no matter how hard Ann tries, she'll never change her Pug into a Golden Retriever. I know, because I've watched many women, including myself, try but fail to change their men. You can't change the spots on a dog. The same applies to men.

For twenty years, I've studied dogs and men and have come to realize that they resemble each other in many ways, including behavior, temperament, and appearance. When I meet a man, I watch him to see which breed of dog he most closely resembles. And even though many men I've interviewed think they're mixed breeds, I can always find a specific dog breed to match them. It is also true that each man is a combination of all the breeds. Every man has a bit of the "hound" in him as well as the "terrier," "herder," and "toy."

My obsession with dogs began when I was eleven months old. The first word I spoke, aside from "Mom," was when I pointed to the dog next door and said "bup" for puppy dog. When I was twelve my parents said I could have a dog, so I read all the dog breed books I could find and memorized the characteristics of all the major breeds. I picked a Samoyed, and I was in love.

Years later I grew more interested in boys and realized they had a lot in common with what I loved most in life—dogs. I noticed one man I dated, happy-go-lucky David, would do whatever I asked him to do—much like a Labrador Retriever. And the next man, Chris, was as unpredictable as some Doberman Pinschers I've known. I never knew when he might snap at me.

After many unsuccessful relationships, I decided to apply what I knew about dogs to find the man for me. At 27, I succeeded in doing just that. I met a Borzoi man and realized that we matched as perfectly as I did with the Borzoi dogs that have lived with me. Since I used this ability to find the perfect husband, and since I understand both men and dogs so well, I decided to write a book giving other women the tools to choose the right men for them.

I want you to know the happiness of being with the man who is right for you. This book was designed to encourage women to be more discriminating when selecting a man, since there are so many breeds of men from which to choose. With the questionnaires in the next chapter, you will better understand your needs, and, using the detailed breed descriptions, you will recognize the breed for you. When you meet a man, you'll know if he's a Great Dane man, a Shih Tzu man, or a Poodle man. Those of you currently in a relationship will understand how to "train" and "handle" your breed of man. This will surely become one of your most valuable tools to developing a harmonious relationship with your man.

Now let's take a closer look at the commonalities between man and dog. Then take the survey and find out which breed of man is best for you and what breeds of men you have in your life.

1

UNDERSTANDING WHY MEN ARE LIKE DOGS

W HY WOULD we want to compare men to dog breeds? Isn't that a bit demeaning? Not when you consider how wonderful dogs are! Men and dogs have much in common. Both are loyal, loving, and affectionate with those they bond to. They protect, comfort, and amuse us. And they usually try to please us, even if we don't recognize their ways of doing so.

Dogs are quite human in their expression of emotions. Do you have a dog, or have you been around dogs? When we return home, how do our dogs behave? Usually with joy, right? They jump on us, spin in circles, and wag their tails. So it's hard to deny that they are happy to see us. What happens when you leave or when an owner dies? I've observed dogs expressing their sorrow through howling or refusing to eat, and there are countless stories of dogs dying within days or

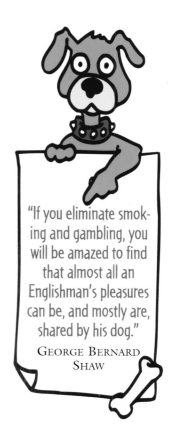

"If you eliminate smoking and gambling, you will be amazed to find that almost all an Englishman's pleasures can be, and mostly are, shared by his dog."
GEORGE BERNARD SHAW

"All knowledge, the totality of all questions and all answers, is contained in the dog."

KAFKA

weeks of their owners. Most dog owners insist that dogs exhibit the same emotions as we do.

We also share more than emotions with dogs. Sit in the park and observe them with their owners. A young blond man wearing shorts and a T-shirt tosses a Frisbee to his lean, white-and-tan Australian Shepherd who leaps high in the air, grabbing the Frisbee and returning it to his master. Across the pond a rambunctious little boy pokes his stick in a hole while his Jack Russell Terrier runs circles around him until given the opportunity to dig into the hole. Sitting on the park bench is a gruff-looking man smoking his cigar and reading the paper. Lying on the ground by his feet is a bulldog who looks every bit as contrary as his owner. You may have noticed there is a recognizable pattern—dogs and their owners often look and behave like one another. Perhaps one of the reasons people appreciate dogs comes from our similarities.

If we go back in time, thousands of years ago, we know that it didn't take much for men and dogs to appreciate each other's company. Dogs helped man on the hunt, and man let the dogs have a share of the game. Over time men bred dogs to complement themselves and their interests. The breeds became more defined and more specialized, as did men. The reason I'm comparing men to dogs, instead of women to dogs, is because men, more than women, developed most of the breeds. Men were imitating themselves with the different breeds. Dog breeds were engineered to assist man, not woman. We can assume that since men bred dogs to assist them, they were encouraging traits they admired in themselves. If dog breeds are a reflection of man himself, why were so many different breeds of dogs created?

HISTORY OF THE BREEDS

Each breed of man was developed to perform certain tasks. Early man was a hunter. He was built for speed, agility, strength, and intelligence . . . qualities he emphasized when he developed the Greyhound and Saluki dogs. Over time, large, intimidating men found their niche in guarding and in war. Thus the Mastiff and other similar breeds arose.

Nomadic man continued to copy himself with breeds that were the precursors to Collies and other herding dogs. Like the men who bred them, these dogs would protect and herd man's livestock. Later, more defined roles arose, such as Siberian Huskies and other sled dogs to traverse snow and ice-covered regions, Rottweilers to pull carts and protect goods, Saint Bernards for rescue, Bulldogs and other tough dogs to fight, and Terriers to get rid of vermin. All of these breeds performed tasks that men, not women, primarily conducted.

Leisure time and an easy lifestyle, particularly among men of class and wealth, meant more refinements in both men and dogs. This is most evident in the hunt. Hunting dogs were bred with more specific traits. Pointers and Setters were bred to stand perfectly still and point to the game. Retrievers and Spaniels were developed that could flush and then gently carry birds in their mouths to man. The wealthy, who could afford the luxury of leisure, copied themselves in other ways with companion dogs, such as the Maltese, Shih Tzu, and other small lap dogs. These dogs, like their masters, enjoyed being pampered and waited on.

In our modern world, men have rapidly adapted to fit their ever-changing environment, and so have dogs. Some breeds, such as the Cocker Spaniel, that have become more leisurely oriented, like many men, can no longer even remember how to hunt. Certain breeds of dogs and men, such as some Labradors, have dispensed with their hunting days and now aid the handicapped. As man changes, so do dogs. Dogs continue to be a reflection of man. That is why we can compare the two. One way to view both men and dogs is by the breed classifications.

When you know a man's breed, then you will know how he evolved, and you will know his true nature. That is when you can understand that his behavior is innate and, therefore, allow him to be what he is—his natural personality. For instance, I married a Borzoi man who tends to be independent. There are times when he requires space. If I try to cuddle up to him on the sofa at that time, he may ignore me. It would be easy to feel hurt or offended by this action, but since he's a Borzoi, I know this is typical behavior, and he doesn't mean it as an insult. I let it be, and when he's ready he'll cuddle.

If you try to change a man, he'll snarl and fight you every inch of the way. You'll be frustrated, and he'll feel like a failure, since he can't make you happy by being who he is. So know the breed that's right for you. You'll find your relationship will take much less effort when you let your man be who he is.

BREED GROUPS

The first step toward examining the breeds of men is through the seven basic groups. These groups are based mainly on men's abilities and interests. Different countries use different methods for classifying dog breeds. This book follows the system used in the United States by the American Kennel Club.

There is a short summation about each group, which is found at the beginning of each chapter. This book lists 42 different breeds. In most dog books, you can find over 150 breeds, and Desmond Morris's book *Dogs* lists over 1,000. Since many breeds are similar, I chose a good number of the well-known ones to represent the majority of breeds of men.

Are you ready to find the breed for you? If you are single, this next chapter will help you recognize your "Mr. Right." If you already have a boyfriend or are married, this chapter will reveal your needs in a relationship. This is valuable information. Once you know your expectations and your man's abilities, you can find a way to blend your differences and create a harmonious relationship.

BREED GROUPS

1) Herding Group
2) Sporting Group
3) Hound Group
4) Working Group
5) Terrier Group
6) Toy Group
7) Non-Sporting
   Group

2

How to Determine the Right Breed for You

What Are Your Needs?

HERE ARE TWO methods to determine what breed of man is best for you. One, answer the questions in this chapter and then use Chart 1 to locate your breed of man. Second, look at Charts 2–11. Based on the factors that are most important to you, find the breeds of men who have those qualities. For instance, if you want a man to be excellent with children, then locate the breeds of men that rate High with children. If the second most important criterion is his level of affection with you, then find a breed of man rated High in that category that was also rated High with children. Continue that process using all of the charts to find the breed of your dreams. I would also encourage you to use a combination of the questions and the charts. The questions help flush out who you are

"In order to really enjoy a dog, one doesn't merely try to train him to be semi-human. The point of it is to open oneself to the possibility of becoming partly a dog."

EDWARD HOAGLAND

and what is important to you, and the charts provide a means to prioritize certain characteristics in a man.

There are many factors to consider before choosing a man. Six of these are listed below:

1. level of experience a woman should have to choose that particular breed
2. how that breed will behave with children
3. the amount of exercise required
4. the activity level for that breed
5. how easy that breed is to train
6. how that breed will react to strangers

These six factors make up the basis for the questions in this chapter and the next chapter. To determine your requirements for a man, answer the questions for each of the six factors. Answer each question as truthfully as possible. The answers to these questions will reveal your needs and desires in a relationship. To pick the right breed of man, you must be completely honest about yourself. This is your relationship we're talking about, and you can't take it lightly because your future happiness depends on accuracy. If you are currently in a relationship, be especially careful not to answer the questions to imitate the man you are with. Even if you love him and think he's "the one," you need to be objective. Don't kid yourself.

After you examine your responses you will be closer to picking the right breed of man for yourself or knowing if the man you are currently with is the right one. If the breed for you and the breed of man you are currently with differ, you can still have a successful relationship. With an understanding of your differences you will be better equipped to recognize where your expectations and his abilities vary. Thus you can use the material provided to approach him with love and respect for who he is.

1. THE LEVEL OF EXPERIENCE A WOMAN SHOULD HAVE TO CHOOSE THAT PARTICULAR BREED.

The first factor, the level of experience a woman should have to be in a relationship with a man of a particular breed, rates breeds as either fine for novice women or for experienced women only. A novice woman has either had little experience with men, or the experiences she has had were negative. An experienced woman is accustomed to men's ways and can remain strong and confident of herself regardless of the behavior of the man she is with. If a breed of man is for the experienced woman, it's either because he exhibits a high level of independence, aloofness, stubbornness, or has the potential to become physically or verbally aggressive.

List 1

YES   NO

1) Did you grow up with a father or father figure?
2) Do you have any brothers?
3) Did you grow up around men you were close to? (i.e. grandfathers, uncles, neighbors, etc.)
4) Did you have male friends in high school or college?
5) Have you dated more than five men in your life?
6) Have you read books about men from a male perspective? (i.e. *Men Are From Mars, Women Are From Venus* or *What Really Works With Men*)
7) Have men acknowledged you for your understanding of them?

List 2

YES   NO

1) Have you ever felt emotionally or physically abused by a man?
2) Have you ever felt controlled by a man against your wishes or better judgment?

If you answered YES to five or more questions from List 1 and NO to both questions in List 2, then consider yourself an "experienced woman"

If you had four or fewer YES responses from List 1, OR you answered YES to either of the questions from List 2, then you are a novice and may want to avoid any breed that requires an experienced woman. There are, however, a few exceptions to this rule, such as:

If you feel confident in your ability to handle a relationship with an extremely independent, aloof, or stubborn man, or a man who has the potential to be aggressive. If you could handle an independent man but not a potentially aggressive man, then check Chart 3 in the back of the book. This chart separates breeds by characteristics such as independence versus stubbornness versus aggressiveness.

If you have any doubts about yourself, then stick to the breeds in the novice category. I realize that some women are attracted to men such as the Rottweiler because of their "tough guy" look or their strength, and a novice breed like the Golden Retriever may not appeal to them. If this is the case, consider breeds of men such as the Boxer, Bulldog, or Great Dane who have the look, are strong, and are also fine for novice women.

2. HOW THAT BREED WILL BEHAVE WITH CHILDREN.

Another consideration is how a man behaves with children. Will he make a good father? Will he be actively involved in the child-rearing or leave it to you? Does he even want children? Does he have the potential to get rough with children?

This can be a tricky subject because there are exceptions within each breed. As a general rule, though, you will find the following to be accurate in regard to children:

— HIGH: a man in this category will usually handle children of all ages with ease. He will take responsibility in raising the children. He may insist on having children.

— MODERATE: a man in this category will know how to relate with older children. He may not be as adept at handling young ones, especially for long periods of time. The moment they start to cry he may hand them to someone else. He may not want to be active in the child-rearing department. He may or may not want to have children. You'll have to ask him and study him to find out.

— LOW: a man in this category has the potential to snap at a child and possibly get too rough. This may be less likely to occur if he has grown up around younger children. Some breeds in this category can also be excellent with children. If you are interested in a man who fits in this category, watch him with children very closely, especially when he thinks no one is watching. A man in this category may be less likely to want children than those designated Moderate or High.

The following test will give you some guidance in choosing the appropriate breed of man. But also keep in mind that any man, regardless of his breed, may not want to have children. Have you ever met a man who was great with children but didn't have any? There are men like that, so you may have to ask a man what he wants and observe him to tell if he's speaking the truth. It's best to know what he wants or will choose before you get in a serious relationship or marry him.

LIST 3

                    YES   NO
1) Do you have young children still living at home?
2) Do you want to have children?
3) Do you want the man in your life to like children?
4) Can you be content as the primary caregiver until the
   the children are older?

If you answered YES to the first two or three questions then pick a breed that says High. If you answered YES to all four questions, then you could possibly work with breeds of men that are also in the Moderate category. However, you will find a larger percentage of men in the Moderate category who do not want children. If you are interested in a man in the Moderate category then continue with the questions in List 4.

If you responded with a NO to the first three questions and YES to question 4, in List 3, then Low could also work. For the woman who does not want children, be cautious before choosing a man from the High group. Some of these breeds will definitely want to have children if they do not yet have children.

If you are interested in a breed of man with a rating of Moderate or Low, and you answered YES to any of the questions listed above, then ask the man you are interested in the following questions:

LIST 4 QUESTIONS TO ASK A MAN

                    YES   NO
1) Were you raised around younger children?
2) Do you like children?
3) Do you want to have children?

If he answers YES then you can possibly make the relationship work. To be on the cautious side, observe him with children of all ages and see how he behaves. Actions speak louder than words. You must be cautious because some men will tell you whatever they think you want to hear. But their actions rarely lie.

3. THE AMOUNT OF EXERCISE REQUIRED.

All breeds of men require exercise for their physical and mental health but some breeds more than others. A few breeds of men, rated HIGH, need exercise every day and may crave time outdoors. The breeds rated MODERATE enjoy physical activity, and a good workout a few times a week will do. Other breeds rated LOW may not need as much exercise, especially if they lead an active lifestyle, or they may prefer not to exercise. Regardless of how much exercise a man needs, you will usually be well matched if your needs are similar. If you enjoy the outdoors and exercise on a consistent basis, would you prefer a man interested in joining you or a man who spends his spare time watching TV? Chances are the outdoor man who will ride bikes with you, go camping, and maybe lift weights at the gym will be the better match. To determine your exercise lifestyle, answer the following questions:

LIST 5

                            YES   NO
1) Do you enjoy and have to exercise every day on a consistent basis?
2) Do you exercise a few times a week on a consistent basis?
3) Do you rarely get exercise?
4) Do you have to force yourself to exercise and would prefer not to?

If you answered YES to question 1, rate yourself High. If you answered YES to question 2, rate yourself Moderate. And if you answered YES to questions 3 or 4, then rate yourself Low on the exercise scale. When choosing a man, examine his exercise lifestyle and see how compatible you are.

4. THE ACTIVITY LEVEL FOR THAT BREED.

Activity level is different than exercise. Some breeds may not require much exercise, but they may be very active like the Jack Russell Terrier.

This breed of man may stay up till midnight playing games on the computer and then be up before dawn to fix the hot water heater before going to work early so he can write up his latest proposal for the boss. A High rating indicates a busy, active man who rarely slows down.

A Moderate rating describes a man who goes back and forth between high activity and low activity. He can go a mile a minute and then relax by meditating, reading a book, or watching TV without thinking about a million other projects and things to do.

A Low rating points to a man who takes his time and is extremely laid back. He may be very accomplished in his career and work hard if he has to. But, given a choice, he will take life easy, doing activities that he enjoys and doing them at his own pace.

The following test will assist you in determining your activity level and, therefore, the activity level in a man that may suit you best. You must decide if you want a man who matches you in activity level or one who acts as a counter to you. For instance, if you're a low-activity woman, you might prefer a man who will take up the slack and do the dishes, mow the yard, and fix the stairs. So a man with a Moderate or maybe even a High rating might be perfect for you. On the other hand, if you like taking life slow and would prefer a man who moves at your pace, then pick a man rated Low.

LIST 6

                        YES   NO

1) Are you a go-getter with a busy schedule?
2) Are you fidgety: do you bite your nails, twirl your hair, tap your feet, or any other activity to keep you moving?
3) Do you wish others would speed up?
4) Do you go back and forth between busy and slow?
5) Can you complete a project and relax before starting the next?
6) Do you walk at an average speed, neither rushing nor dragging?
7) Do active people, moving in high gear, annoy or tire you?
8) Do you prefer to lie around and spend most of your time that way?
9) Do you prefer to go at your own pace?

If you answered YES to questions 1, 2, and 3, you are probably a High activity woman. If you answered YES to questions 4, 5 and 6, chances are you rate Moderate on the active scale. And if you answered YES to questions 7, 8 and 9, you are probably a Low activity woman. If your answers were mixed, decide which level best describes you—High, Moderate or Low. Now that you know what you are, what do you want in a man? Look at the questions above and decide what response you would like him to have.

5. HOW EASY THAT BREED IS TO TRAIN.

One of the most important choices you will make regards ease in training a man. The word *train* does not imply what some people think—that we as women would control a man or make him do something he does not want to do. Instead *train* means we understand and appreciate what motivates a man and encourage behavior that we prefer through positive reinforcement. Some men respond well to praise, others require more substantial rewards, and some will refuse a request regardless of the motivation we use. However a man may respond, it is important for you to love and honor him, finding rewards that speak to him and are easy for you to give.

Most men are not that complicated, but that's not to say they're all easy to train. Some breeds were designed to be independent, such as the Bloodhound. Independence enables a member of this breed to follow a trail on his own. It does not require someone telling him where to turn and when to stop. Unfortunately, this sometimes makes the Bloodhound harder to train. With this breed, and some of the others, training may require more creativity and take more time. Also note that intelligence is not *always* equated with ease of training. In the case of the Dachshund man, he is extremely intelligent and learns fast but can be somewhat challenging to train because of his stubborn nature.

If a man receives a rating of High, you can usually count on him to do what you ask, when you ask. He will probably have a strong desire to make you happy.

A man in the Moderate category may take more coaxing than the High rated breed. For instance, if you ask this man to wash the car, he might look at you as if you had asked him to do it with a toothbrush. Then he'll sigh or moan and eventually wash the car. Or he might respond eagerly to your request but not get around to it until you've reminded him three or four times. It might take some big reward like going to see some action/adventure shoot 'em up movie rather than the romantic comedy you wanted to see.

The man who rates Low on the training scale can be a challenge with a capital C. Men in this category are not trying to be difficult; they just operate differently. Think of a cat. When you call one does it always come? I can look my cat Sheer Khan right in the eye, call him, and still have him look at me as if I had said, "Sheer Khan, stay there. Don't move," rather than, "Sheer Khan, here, kitty kitty." These men need major motivation and reward to respond to you. And threats rarely work. In fact, the more you push and pull, the more they resist. The trick is finding the key to motivating a breed of man in this category. You sometimes have to use the process of elimination to find the motivator.

List 7

How would you answer the following statements? YES   NO

1) I want a man who will respond to me and do as I ask right away.
2) I don't want to spend a lot of time trying to understand what motivates a man.
3) A man who does what he wants to do, without thinking about me, exasperates me.
4) I expect a man to know what I want without having to explain everything to him.
5) I respect and honor a man who is independent even if it means doing things his way sometimes.
6) I don't get upset when a man moans or groans after being asked to help out.
7) It's okay if a man takes his time before he does what I ask, so long as he eventually does it.
8) I'm willing to give a little to get a little in return.
9) I can accept a man who ignores me or says no when asked to do something.
10) I'm creative and will spend whatever time it takes to understand the motivation my man needs.
11) I can work with an independent, stubborn man.
12) I'm not very demanding. I'm a low-maintenance woman.

If statements 1 through 4 suits you best, then the breed of man you pick, or the man you are with, should be rated High on the ease of training scale. Statements 5 through 8 reflect a woman who could handle a man with a Moderate rating and possibly a High rating. And statements 9 through 12 would hold true for a woman capable of living with a Low rated man. If you have a mix between High, Moderate and Low, then decide which would be most appropriate for you based on the description of High, Moderate, and Low.

6. How that breed will react to strangers.

The last of the six characteristics involves how each breed of man reacts to strangers. The level of sociability a man possesses may influence his social life and yours. If a particular breed of man immediately welcomes strangers with open arms, he rates High for being very social and outgoing. Or will he be polite but a little distant until he knows someone better? If this is the case he rates Moderate, meaning he takes his time before opening up to someone. Or will he be cautious, shy, or resistant to meeting new people? If YES he rates Low for the tendency to be distant with strangers. Again, when answering the questions be honest about yourself and your needs.

LIST 8

YES   NO

1) Would you prefer a man who makes friends easily and immediately likes everyone he meets?
2) Are you in social situations that require an outgoing, friendly man?
3) Would you prefer a man who is polite to strangers but takes his time warming up to people?
4) Are you comfortable meeting strangers but need time to get to know them?
5) Would you prefer a man who is very shy or cautious with strangers?
6) Are you cautious or shy around strangers and don't feel the need to know them better?

If you answered YES to questions 1 and 2 you should probably pick a breed of man rated High in sociability. YES to questions 3 and 4 indicates a breed rated Moderate. And questions 5 and 6 are representative of a breed rated Low. The possibility exists that you answered the question regarding yourself the opposite of the kind of man you want. Maybe you answered YES to question 1 and YES to question 6. In that case, maybe you would prefer a man who makes up for your reservation with strangers. And that's okay as long as you're aware of your motivation and realize he may like someone before you're ready to.

I know a woman who's moderately social and picked a man rated High. Now she's tired of the parties and all the people. And I know another woman who's with a man rated Low even though she's highly social. She can't get him to attend any parties or get-togethers unless he knows everyone there. If you pick a breed of man, whether he rates High, Moderate, or Low you have to honor his way of handling strangers. You can't change him, and, if you can't accept his behavior, then find a different breed of man.

THE CHART

With the answers to questions 1–6, you may now turn to Chart 1 listing all the breeds of men. Most of the time one or more breeds will be a perfect match. If not, then look for breeds that are off by one ranking. Such as exercise being High whereas you listed Moderate. Sometimes you will have to look for breeds that are off by two. This can still be accurate because even with dog breeds you will find breeds that normally may not be good with children, yet some dogs within those breeds will like children.

If you find a couple or more breeds that could be the one, then read about each of those breeds to decide which one is the best for you. Pay particular attention to the part called Type of Woman. Also make use of Charts 3–11 to prioritize your answers. If Ease of Training and Level of Affection are most important, make sure the breed you're looking at has the score you want.

Now that you know the breed for you, what breeds are the men in your life? What breeds are your husband, boyfriend, father, or friends?

3

WHAT BREED IS HE?

DETERMINING WHAT BREED a man is, whether he is a husband, boyfriend, father, brother, or friend, can be fun. It can be easy if you know the man well. If not, you may need to ask him, close family members, or friends the questions. When asking men these questions, encourage them to be completely honest. Assure them that there are no wrong answers. Every breed is awesome and unique. I encourage men to be proud of who they are, embrace who they are, and not pretend to be something else. If a man is a Poodle, there are plenty of women who would love to be with a Poodle man. It's much better for a Poodle man to be with a woman who loves a Poodle man than to pretend to be a German Shepherd man and spend his life living a lie.

The following are questions to ask a *man*, not a woman, in order to determine what

"God . . . sat down for a moment when the dog was finished in order to watch it . . . and to know that it was good, that nothing was lacking, that it could not have been made better."
RAINER MARIA RILKE

breed he is. Remember, the comparison of men to dog breeds applies to men only.

1. FOR NOVICE OR EXPERIENCED WOMEN

Ask a man: Are you extremely independent, aloof, stubborn, and/or do you have a tendency to be overly assertive, even physically or verbally aggressive?

YES to any of these places him in the *For Experienced Women* category. NO to all of these places him in the *Fine for Novice* category.

2. BEHAVIOR WITH CHILDREN

Do you love children, want to have children, and are you great with children of all ages? If YES then you rank High.

Are you best with older children? Can infants be a challenge? If YES, then put Moderate.

Do children sometimes annoy you to the extent you have to get away from them? Can they get on your nerves if around them for too long? Might you get too rough with them? If YES then put Low, keeping in mind this man may or may not like children.

3. EXERCISE REQUIRED

Do you love to exercise and require it every day or you feel something's missing? If so, put High.

Do you enjoy exercise but a few times a week is enough? Then put Moderate.

Do you prefer not to exercise at all or find that you are so active you require little to no exercise? If so, put Low.

4. LEVEL OF ACTIVITY

Do you constantly stay busy? Do you have multiple projects happening at once? Even when sitting down are you tapping your foot and thinking of a million things at once? If so, put High.

Are you busy, going full speed ahead, and then when you stop, you relax and take it easy by reading a book or watching TV without thinking about everything you have to do? YES means Moderate.

Can you accomplish things when you need to, but, given a choice, you would prefer not to have to do much of anything? A life of leisure would suit you great? If so, put Low.

5. EASE OF TRAINING

If a woman in a relationship with you asks you to do something for her, do you immediately respond? Do you sometimes second-guess her and do what she asks before she asks? If YES, then you are High. However, if you think you are High and women say you don't always understand what they want or what they are asking of you, then put Moderate.

If a woman has to ask you a few times to do something, and you sometimes feel "put out" or complain about her request, then put Moderate.

Do you sometimes not even realize a woman's asked you to do something? Does it bother you or upset you when a woman asks you to do something you don't want to do? Do you behave like a cat, just looking at her or ignoring her when called? Even if you don't mean to be difficult but you answer YES to the above questions, then put Low.

6. SOCIABILITY WITH STRANGERS

Do you enjoy meeting people? Is it easy for you to become fast friends with people you just met? Are you comfortable going to events where you meet new people? If YES, then put High.

Are you polite to strangers but take your time warming up to them? Maybe you wait until you know them better to show them who you are. If so, put Moderate.

Are you shy around strangers, distrust new people, or just not feel a need to meet new people? If YES to any of these, you are Low.

THE CHART

With the answers to questions 1–6, you can determine what breed a man is. Look at the the chart listing all the breeds and these six factors. Usually, one breed will be a match. If not, search for a breed with one, possibly two, factors off. For instance, if a man rates HIGH for exercise, but none of the breeds match, then look for a breed that rates MODERATE for exercise instead. If you find two or more possible breed matches, then read about those breeds to find the perfect match. The *Abilities & Interests* section will reveal a lot about his true nature, so pay particular attention to that description. The next chapter describes the five characteristics attributed to each breed of man, including *Abilities & Interests.*

Each breed is awesome and perfect just the way it is. I would like to see men proud of who they are and eager to show women their true natures. For each breed of man, there is a woman who will love and appreciate that breed. It may take longer for some breeds to find women who are understanding and capable of being in relationships with them. However, it is better to wait and find that woman than to settle for someone who can never be happy with the way a man behaves. Relationships can be easy and joyful when two people come together who truly love, honor, and respect one another.

4
BREED CHARACTERISTICS

F OR EACH BREED of man there is a detailed
description of five major characteristics.
These five characteristics are as follows:
1. Physical Characteristics
2. Abilities and Interests
3. Training
4. Social Skills
5. Type of Woman

1. PHYSICAL CHARACTERISTICS

What will he look like? Will his appearance
draw women to him like a magnet? You might
want to consider this if you're the jealous type.
How does he carry himself—majestic, arrogant,
sad, etc.? Is he particular about his appearance?
Some men want every hair in place while the
next man rarely looks in the mirror. If you don't
know a man that well, this section may help you

I'm a mog. Half man,
half dog. I'm my
own best friend.

"BARF," JOHN
CANDY, *SPACEBALLS*

determine his breed. A Poodle man looks quite different from a Bloodhound man. Recognizing a breed of man requires more imagination than looking at dog breeds, but the more you study them the more you pick up on the similarities.

While writing this book I asked many women to describe their boyfriends' or husbands' characteristics based on the descriptions listed earlier: ease of training, sociability with strangers, etc. Using this list we compared it to the diagram to determine their breed of man. We were consistently amazed at the physical similarities between the man and the dog breed. Sally's husband, a Schnauzer, has eyebrows, a beard and mustache that look just like a Schnauzer dog. Another woman's man doesn't have a lot of hair on his head, but the hair he does have is all over the place like an Old English Sheepdog. He also has the burly body of a Sheepdog. You might have to do some creative thinking to determine a breed of man based on his appearance, but when you know what to look for you can usually see the resemblance.

I would encourage all women to look beyond appearances in choosing a man. It's the inner man that counts more than the outer. At the same time I recognize that a certain type of look may appeal to some women. For instance, if men with a rough façade appeal to you then you may choose breeds such as the Bulldog, Mastiff, Boxer, Pit Bull, Pug, or Rottweiler. Whichever breed you choose be sure he's a good match for you.

2. ABILITIES AND INTERESTS

"Abilities and interests" examines the natural inclinations of each breed of man. This will influence the careers they may be drawn to or their hobbies. Most men have a predisposition for certain traits. For some this may be the ability to track people or for others the ability to remain calm in high-pressure situations. These traits, to a large extent, influence a man's behavior and his preferences.

This section and the training section may be the most important characteristics to consider when choosing a man. Women who don't pay enough attention to this section or don't take it seriously could end up in a disastrous relationship. You could be in trouble if you think you want an Australian Shepherd man because they are good with children, are intelligent, and moderately easy to train, but you ignore the description in *Abilities & Interests.* Listed under *Abilities & Interests,* it says Aussies like to herd, and you may grow weary of being herded to the baseball game, the park, and anywhere else he wants to go.

The key to picking the right man is understanding and acceptance. First, you must understand what drives your man to do the things he does. An Akita man by nature wants to protect. When a strange man tries to pull you out on the dance floor don't be surprised if your Akita man responds in an aggressive manner. This is his nature. It's the way he was bred. If you understand what makes him tick then ask yourself: Can you accept this?

Be completely honest. Could you spend the rest of your life with a man if certain traits or behaviors never change? If the answer is NO, then do not continue the relationship (unless you are already married). The chances that a man will change his behavior on his own or that you will force him to change are slim. An Akita man with a protective tendency may not back down if provoked even if you beg or threaten him.

> Don't pick a breed that has certain characteristics
> you find intolerable.

Another way to protect yourself from picking the wrong man is to watch his actions. A man may tell you you're the most beautiful woman he's ever known, and he'll never want to look at another woman the rest of his life as long as he's with you. However, if he's a sight hound like the Borzoi or Rhodesian Ridgeback, I bet at some time you will catch him looking at other women. It's his nature, and he can't hide it forever. Remember, actions speak louder than words.

3. TRAINING

Training is a term used loosely in this book. I would not claim that a woman *trains* a man. I use it because this book mimics dog breed manuals, and they use the word *train.* I do however agree with the concept that men, like dogs, respond to positive reinforcement. And, as with dogs, you can learn to read your man and understand what motivational technique will elicit the response you want.

Some women tell me they don't believe in manipulating their man, and training sounds manipulative. If we make a man do something against his better judgment or do something that does harm, it is manipulative. It is *not* manipulative if we understand a man and work in alignment with his given nature to encourage certain behaviors and actions that benefit him, the relationship, and ourselves. I give my husband, Lance, a lot of slack because he is a Borzoi who is not easy to train. If something is important to me I've learned to be clear in my communication, offer a good reward, and still allow him the freedom to say no.

Training is as important as abilities and interests when it comes to choosing a man. The first step, know your needs. If you answered the questions in the previous section on training then you know what you want and are capable of handling.

After you make an honest assessment of your needs and you pick one or more breeds as possibilities, you can then look at each breed's training needs to determine what suits you best. Even though both the Weimaraner and the Scottish Terrier are rated Low, their motivations are very different. Rewarding a Weimaraner by playing ball works; the Scottish Terrier, however, may prefer food or praise. So for each breed of man, look at his abilities and interests to know what might appeal to him.

4. SOCIAL SKILLS

Different breeds exhibit different social skills, their behavior ranging from aloof to outgoing. These skills may vary according to the type of relationship a man is involved in. There are four major relationships discussed in this section. The first involves strangers, next is friends, third is children, and last, you, the woman in his life.

Certain breeds of men are so affectionate they immediately glue themselves to a woman. They'll call a woman every two or three hours. And as soon as they finish work they'll expect her to spend every available minute with them. Then there's the extreme opposite breed of man who may be so aloof he spends most of his time on the road traveling and rarely even calls home. See Chart 9 for Level of Affection for each breed.

A man's social skills with the woman in his life may vary from those exhibited with strangers, his friends, and children. If you study a man's actions in different settings you can usually tell what type of social skills he has and understand him better. Observe him with strangers, friends, and family. How does he interact with his mother, sisters, and other women friends? Especially learn about his relationship with his mother when he was a young boy. If you can, find out how he treated previous girlfriends or wives. Looking at all these relationships, you will have a pretty accurate picture of how he'll relate to you over time.

5. TYPE OF WOMAN

This section defines the type of woman best suited for a particular breed of man. The more you and a man have in common, the more you will understand one another, and the more chances the relationship has of succeeding. An athletic woman will usually prefer a man who also likes to ride bikes or go windsurfing with her. A woman who loves children may be happiest with a man who also adores children. And a strong-willed woman may need a man she can respect, a man who can also stand his ground.

Separate interests can also provide diversity in a relationship, as long as you can appreciate your differences and honor them. When it comes to belief systems, it is especially important to examine your ideas about spirituality, family, career, money, and time compared to his ideas.

You have probably heard the saying opposites attract. That may be true, but why? Sometimes women pick men with qualities that they are weak in. For instance, a shy woman may pick a man who is outgoing. Later she may become more outgoing and not feel the need for him, or she may grow weary of his outgoing nature.

Sometimes women choose men who are their opposites as a way to rebel. Kate's father was a minister, and she consistently picked men with notorious reputations as a way to upset her father, thus gaining his attention. The need to rebel eventually decreased and she found a "respectable" man, more like her, and was much happier. Opposites may attract, but over time they may repel.

When we accept and love ourselves for who we are, we can make healthy choices. We can choose men who are like us or not and do so based on our highest good.

Let's meet the wonderful breeds of men.

BREED LEGEND

NOVICE VERSUS EXPERIENCED:

How much knowledge must a woman possess about men in order to be with a particular man? If a man needs a woman with experience, it is because he is extremely stubborn, independent or aggressive (verbally or physically).

BEHAVIOR WITH CHILDREN:

How a man will behave with the little ones.

EXERCISE REQUIRED:

How much physical activity a man requires.

ACTIVITY LEVEL:

How active or busy a man is when it comes to work, rest, and play.

EASE OF TRAINING:

How quickly and eagerly a man responds to a partner's request.

SOCIABILITY WITH STRANGERS:

How a man will respond to unfamiliar persons.

AFFECTION LEVEL:

How loving and attentive a man is in an intimate relationship with his partner.

PLAYFULNESS:

How fun-loving a man can be.

PROTECTIVENESS:

How strong a man's need is to defend himself and others. Need may be based on reality or his perception.

WATCHDOG ABILITY:

How strong a man's need is to recognize and alert others to danger.

🦴 = LOW   🦴 🦴 = MODERATE   🦴 🦴 🦴 = HIGH

5

THE HERDING GROUP

THE HERDING GROUP of men have a strong desire to herd. Some do this intellectually, others physically, and some spiritually. They follow orders extremely well if they respect you and understand you.

AUSTRALIAN SHEPHERD: These guys are energetic herders, putting people and things in their place. They are ready for work or play. Just let them know which.

COLLIE: These gentle, beautiful men can steal your heart. They are fairly laid back but may try to herd you physically, mentally, spiritually, or any other way they can.

GERMAN SHEPHERD: These watchful guys are very protective. They are multitalented and can succeed at just about anything they attempt.

OLD ENGLISH SHEEPDOG: These guys love to watch over while reclining. They'll also herd if they think something or somebody needs direction.

THE AUSTRALIAN SHEPHERD MAN

QUALITIES:

- HERDING INSTINCT
- HARDWORKING
- INDEPENDENT BUT CAN FOLLOW ORDERS
- ENJOYS THE OUTDOORS AND SPORTS

FOR EXPERIENCED WOMEN DUE TO: INDEPENDENCE

Behavior with children:	🦴🦴🦴
Exercise required:	🦴🦴
Activity level:	🦴🦴
Ease of training:	🦴🦴 or 🦴🦴🦴
Sociability with strangers:	🦴🦴🦴
Affection level:	🦴🦴
Playfulness:	🦴🦴🦴
Protectiveness:	🦴🦴
Watchdog ability:	🦴🦴🦴

PHYSICAL CHARACTERISTICS: Most people are unfamiliar with Australian Shepherd men. When they see one they may think he's a mixed breed. He's not a mutt, but he does have an unusual look resembling a bountiful mix of many breeds of men. The Australian Shepherd man is built for quick moves, and his agility shows in his lithe body frame.

ABILITIES & INTERESTS: By nature, the Australian Shepherd man is a herder. He will work hard to keep others in their place or move them from place to place. He performs best when directed by someone else but does well managing many people under him. The Australian Shepherd man has a lot of energy, which he will expend on sports, studies, or whatever his passion may be. Many people find it hard to keep up with him. He can spend all day at school or work and still feel like a game of Frisbee or golf in the evening. When he decides to relax, he can really let go. Australian Shepherds are very intelligent and great at problem-solving. They're creative thinkers and thus are capable of any career that they put their energy and attention into. Their herding instinct must be allowed to come out or they will feel off-purpose.

TRAINING: Although the Australian Shepherd man is very intelligent, he still may be a challenge to train. A woman who understands the needs of an

Aussie and works with him will find him easy to train. This means allowing him to do his "herding thing" and also playing with him. An Aussie man can also be challenging, though, because he is clever and may find ways to slip out of things. Loyalty is the Australian Shepherd man's strong suit. Deep down inside, an Australian Shepherd man longs to please those he bonds with. If you honor him and approach him with love and kindness, he'll be easy to train and very obedient.

SOCIAL SKILLS: Australian Shepherd men are wary of strangers, and they need to understand a person before deciding whether or not they like or trust him. When sociability is required they can be friendly. If an Australian Shepherd man doesn't trust someone, he can be very protective, and he'll not let harm come to anyone he loves. He may not be the biggest or the strongest of men, but he has courage and tenacity when needed. And once an Australian Shepherd man accepts someone, he can make an outstanding friend. In the family setting, an Australian Shepherd man will love and be devoted to those he bonds with. He can be good with children. Remember the herding instinct! If he doesn't have an outlet, he may use it on the children, and they may resent his need to control when they get older. In a relationship, an Aussie man can be affectionate and loyal with the woman he bonds to. He may try to herd her, but, if he is well trained, he will do this only when it is in her best interest.

TYPE OF WOMAN: The best woman for an Australian Shepherd man will allow him plenty of outdoor time. She'll encourage him to herd in a way that suits him or benefits her, but will stand her ground and not let him herd her, especially as the breed is given to, using annoying and painful nips. She'll give him space to run and feel free, understanding that he could become destructive if bored or if he feels cooped up. Recognizing his need for companionship with her and with his friends, she'll enjoy spending time with him or allowing him time with friends.

TYPICAL AUSTRALIAN SHEPHERD MAN: Michael's story, told by his wife, Barbara:

My husband and I work together. He's the representative for a number of nutritional products, and work is a priority for him. His passion is educating folks about nutrition and supporting them in choosing healthier lifestyles. While Michael is out in the field, I do much of the paperwork and organizational work. At the same time I take care of the housework, our thirteen-year-old daughter's busy schedule, and assisting my parents and other friends. Most of the time I'm going at full speed.

On one such occasion I reached the boiling point. Michael walked in announcing, "I'm going to go play golf."

No way, I thought, and I told him, "No, Michael, I need you. I am so overwhelmed I can't take it anymore."

In his gentle, but firm and unyielding way he said, "Barbara, go change your clothes, you're going with me."

"Michael, you're not listening to me. I have so much to do, you have to stay here and help me out!"

Again in that authoritative way he said, "You're going with me."

Fine, I thought, I'll go. Well, my Australian Shepherd knows how to herd me. As soon as we hit the golf course, with the sun shining and a gentle breeze blowing, I felt all my anxiety melt away. Why was I so stressed? All those things that troubled me before seemed mere trifles. I could handle them later, no problem. I'm a strong-willed woman, and I sometimes refuse to let my husband herd me, but, when I relinquish control, he often seems to know what I need even before I do.

Famous Australian Shepherd Man: Tom Hanks in *Saving Private Ryan*

Tom Hanks obediently follows orders to find Private Ryan even though he questions the mission itself. He's a master at keeping his men together. In one scene the group is close to splitting up, but he cleverly herds them back together by revealing a secret. After grueling battles and travels, Hanks keeps going, staying awake even when the others fall into exhausted sleep.

QUALITIES:

DEVOTED AND LOYAL
GENTLE, QUIET, AND STRONG
COVERT HERDERS
SENSITIVE

FINE FOR NOVICE WOMEN

Behavior with children:

Exercise required:

Activity level:

Ease of training:

Sociability with strangers:

Affection level:

Playfulness:

Protectiveness:

Watchdog ability:

PHYSICAL CHARACTERISTICS: Collie men are very handsome and catch people's eye. They have a friendly, open look about them and a great smile. They are particular about their appearance and will take time to stay well groomed—most of the time. Suits look great on these men, although they generally prefer nice casual dress.

ABILITIES & INTERESTS: Collie men are excellent at herding people, whether they herd them to ideas, places, or philosophies and beliefs. Gentle herders, most people are not aware they are being herded or do not mind being herded. These men make excellent eye contact and are great communicators. They work well with others and follow orders gladly—most of the time. While they are not overly independent, they can think independently when needed. They can be protective and have a sixth sense for danger. Usually, however, a fight has to come to them. They do not go looking for trouble. Collie men like to kick back, enjoy life by reading, watching television, enjoying nature and other leisure activities. Collie men are also very playful and intelligent, so they enjoy games using the mind as well as the physical body. They enjoy most sports and prefer to join others, but, if need be, they can be content exercising on their own.

TRAINING: A Collie man is usually easy to train because he wants to please. He is intelligent and knows how to concentrate. The biggest challenge is his desire to relax and do things in his time frame. This can be overcome with a lot of praise and some reward. Incorporating play and using his herding instinct will make training easier. Due to his sensitive nature, he should never be treated harshly. Criticism will make him despondent and less willing to try and please. It is important in this breed to build confidence. Let him know how wonderful he is and how much you respect him, and he'll respond so much better.

SOCIAL SKILLS: In a social setting with new people, the Collie man can be very polite and well mannered. He will, however, take his time getting to know someone. And unless the new acquaintance truly interests him or there is something in it for him, the Collie man may choose to ignore him. Once he accepts someone, he can be extremely gregarious and playful. He will prefer having a wide circle of friends and some that are very close. He works well with others and will be a team player when needed. He is also quite capable of working by himself, starting a project and then leading others to it. Collie men can be a real mix with children: some are excellent with all children; some are good with older children but not with infants; and others will even snap at children and get rough in their herding of children. Actions are the key to knowing how a Collie man will respond to children. Watch him carefully. In a relationship, he can be affectionate, loyal, loving, and devoted. Just be prepared for his desire to herd you.

TYPE OF WOMAN: The woman for a Collie man will appreciate his intense need to herd; either her or others. She knows he may move at a slow pace when he's not herding. She'll be gentle with him and very loving, realizing that what she gives to him she will receive back times one hundred. She'll be playful and fun-loving, and she'll enjoy board games and outdoor physical activities. If children are important to her, she'll pay attention to his behavior with them.

TYPICAL COLLIE MAN: Rob's story, as told by himself:

I never thought of myself as a herder. I pictured myself as a go-with-the-flow kind of guy. I thought I went along with others, more than leading the way. And I liked this picture of myself. I could even say I was attached to this idea. But one day, I paid attention to my actions and my thoughts, and what I saw surprised me, actually upset me. It upset me because it wasn't who I thought I was, and how could I spend twenty-four hours a day with myself and not know myself? Which then brought the question to mind—who am I?

This introspective process began when I started paying attention to my actions. When my friends and I were together, and we were uncertain where to go or what to do next, I was the one who decided for the group. I gave gentle nudges; I wasn't bossy or controlling, but consistently I was the one herding the others. I couldn't decide if I liked what I saw, especially when it seemed at odds with my self-imposed identity, until one day . . .

I heard that Sherri's cat had died. Sherri and I were good friends and I knew that this cat, Rhada, was her "baby." They had been together for eighteen years—through many moves, a few boyfriends, and tears of joy and pain. She could barely talk when I called. I asked if she would like me to come over, and between sobs she said yes. At Sherri's house I saw Rhada's body wrapped carefully in a silk scarf. Sherri was at a loss for dealing with Rhada's body. She didn't want to let go. The thought of burying her brought more intense sobbing. I gently took charge.

"Sherri, I know a place that cremates pets. My mom took her dog there. At this place they will put Rhada in a beautiful cedar box with a gold plaque on top bearing her name. I'll take you there and handle everything. Would you like that?"

She nodded yes and we left. The place had a parlor, like a funeral home. The people were caring and kind. We left Rhada there, and the next day I delivered her boxed-up ashes to Sherri. A few days later Sherri called me.

"Rob, thank you. I'm so grateful to you for stepping in and gently directing me. You took charge when I felt lost, and having Rhada's ashes has comforted me. I had no idea it would make such a difference for me in coping with her death. I feel blessed having you in my life."

So, I am a herder. And now I like that I am a herder. Maybe, if I pay close attention, I'll discover more about myself that I don't know, and I will grow to love those qualities as well.

FAMOUS COLLIE MAN: Matt Damon as John Grady Cole in *All the Pretty Horses*

As a young man John Cole is eager to escape his humdrum life and travel to Mexico. He wants to work on a big cattle ranch, appropriate for a Collie's herding instinct. Along the way he and his partner bump into a scrawny, younger troublemaker. Despite his partner's misgivings, John feels sorry for the kid and decides to help him, which turns out to be a mistake. When John falls for the rancher's daughter, his loyalty to her creates even more challenges. Throughout the movie, John follows his heart and remains loyal to those he loves.

THE GERMAN SHEPHERD MAN

Qualities:

Strong herding instinct

Multitalented

Take-charge attitude

Protective, sometimes overly so

FOR EXPERIENCED WOMEN DUE TO: AGGRESSIVENESS

Behavior with children: 🦴🦴🦴

Exercise required: 🦴🦴

Activity level: 🦴🦴🦴

Ease of training: 🦴🦴 or 🦴🦴🦴🦴

Sociability with strangers:

Affection level: 🦴🦴

Playfulness: 🦴

Protectiveness: 🦴🦴🦴

Watchdog ability: 🦴🦴🦴

PHYSICAL CHARACTERISTICS: German Shepherd men are very attractive. If one passes by, chances are you'll take a second look. They have well-proportioned bodies that are large but not bulky. A German Shepherd man carries himself with an air of confidence and has a look in his eyes that says, "I know something you don't." It's this air of mystery that women are often attracted to.

ABILITIES & INTERESTS: German Shepherds are by nature protective and can also be controlling. They may try to herd others physically or mentally. Few breeds are as versatile as the German Shepherd man. He's strong, agile, controlled, intelligent, brave, and consistent. But caution is needed because there are many imitations out there. German Shepherd men are very popular, so there are men who pretend to be German Shepherds. A true, well-bred German Shepherd man is extremely intelligent. He learns quickly and retains what he learns. He excels in jobs that require agility, strength, and problem-solving. The military looks for and values German Shepherd men, as do the police force and fire department. They are also excellent in emergency situations where they will search out and rescue those in need. They can remain calm in the most harrowing situations. German Shepherd men also make excellent companions for the disabled. Their patience, intelligence, and calm dispositions make them excellent guides for those who are physically impaired. German Shepherd men enjoy exercise of all kinds. They are content by themselves and can also enjoy group sports.

TRAINING: Training a German Shepherd man is easy if you are confident, can stand your ground, and do not get overly rough with him. Most of all, treat him with respect. From the moment you first meet, you must be clear and consistent. Let him know what you expect of him. Don't make him guess. He's extremely intelligent and wants to please. Don't be upset if he complains a little, and allow him the freedom to sometimes say no to your requests. Work with him, not against him. He will follow orders from authority figures he respects. If respect is missing, however, you'll have an unruly, possibly overbearing man on your hands. If he becomes aggressive, and he may, seek help.

SOCIAL SKILLS: A German Shepherd man may be wary of strangers. If so, take time introducing him to your family and friends. Don't push him into social settings too soon. Although some German Shepherd men can be outgoing, don't expect it of him, and don't try to change him. He will have a few close friends that he knows he can trust, and with them he will be fairly open. He can also be very private even with those close to him. The German Shepherd man makes a good family man. He is loyal and devoted to those he loves. He can be very gentle and loving with children of all ages. If you want a protective man for you or your children, he's your man. If threatened, he will not hesitate to attack. Sometimes he may become a little overprotective. In a committed relationship, he can be affectionate and very devoted.

TYPE OF WOMAN: The best woman for a German Shepherd man is intelligent, confident, able to stand her ground and is not easily intimidated. Women who come on too strong or want to dominate and control a man should be cautious. If a woman pushes him too hard, he may push back even harder. She will appreciate his many talents, interests, and dedication to work. When he stays late at the office, she'll respect him for it rather than complain about it, or she'll get creative and find ways to draw him back home.

TYPICAL GERMAN SHEPHERD MAN: Rod's story, told by his wife, Isabella:

Rod is big, handsome, and definitely a herder. The grandkids call him Big Dog. I remember when we first fell in love some 25 years ago. I wasn't quite divorced from my Australian Shepherd husband, although the divorce was in the works. My German Shepherd man showed up at my house one day and said he had rented a new home for me down the street a ways. Now it is true that I was head over heels in love with the German Shepherd man, but it is also true that I had no intention of setting up a home with him. Also known as the dog of love, he seemed a little dangerous to me. The kind of man I might want to share adventure with but not necessarily build a nest with.

He picked up my typewriter and carried it out to his truck along with a draft of the play we were writing together. Later he told me he had known I would go where my typewriter went, so he packed it first. Leaning against a door jamb, I watched him walk into my bedroom, take a suitcase out of my closet and start packing my things. I was stunned. I sat on the edge of my bed as he scooped out my neatly folded clothes and dropped them by the drawerful into a suitcase.

When I finally found my voice, I said, "I need to think about this."

He said, "Isabella, you can think about it for the rest of your life. But you are going to think about it while you're living with me."

I was being herded. I am a strong-willed woman. How was this happening? What was this power he held over me? I was impressed, actually swept away by his decisiveness. I am the type of person who weighs pros and cons. I deliberate. I hesitate. It has been both liberating and at times frightening living with someone who makes decisions quickly and then acts upon them immediately. My German Shepherd can move through obstacles much like a comic book hero, a daring attribute that can be either creative or destructive. That is part of the attraction. I know he won my heart with the intensity of his vision and his power to act on his belief that we were meant to be together.

In the balance of our relationship, I have raised his ability to pause and analyze, and he has increased my ability to act on intuition. It's a good trade: I bring depth, he brings high adventure. I adore my Shepherd.

FAMOUS GERMAN SHEPHERD MAN: Sean Connery in *Entrapment*

Sean Connery is the perfect German Shepherd man in *Entrapment* because he is handsome, exceptionally intelligent, agile, loyal, and talented. He cleverly figures out how to steal a heavily-guarded Chinese mask. During the heist, he calmly directs his partner to move through a laser obstacle that she cannot see. Sean is slow to trust strangers, and even with friends and acquaintances he remains wary. He grows to love and, in the end, is loyal to the person he respects most.

QUALITIES:

GENTLE HERDER
WATCHFUL OVER OTHERS
TAKES HIS TIME
UNINTENTIONALLY COMIC

FOR EXPERIENCED WOMEN DUE TO: INDEPENDENCE AND STUBBORNNESS

Behavior with children: 🦴 🦴 🦴

Exercise required: 🦴 🦴

Activity level: 🦴 🦴

Ease of training: 🦴

Sociability with strangers: 🦴 🦴

Affection level: 🦴 🦴 🦴

Playfulness: 🦴 🦴

Protectiveness: 🦴 🦴

Watchdog ability: 🦴 🦴

PHYSICAL CHARACTERISTICS: The Old English Sheepdog man has a shuffling gait, similar to a bear's. At first glance, you may think he would be clumsy, but he's actually quite agile and graceful for his size. Wooly and unkempt, Old English Sheepdog men are not usually concerned about their appearance. Even if they have very little hair, it will often be in disarray and their pants may not match their jackets. They're not trying to be creative dressers. They just don't pay attention to visual details. And they'll wear something regardless of how old or out of date it may be. Unless someone else buys them new socks, you'll probably find holes in theirs.

ABILITIES & INTERESTS: The Sheepdog's main instinct is to herd and direct people. He will be good in positions of authority such as teaching and management. People will look up to and respect his leadership methods because he tends to "watch over" rather than "rule over" others. A Sheepdog man can be content spending hours observing events around him. You might think he's asleep or not paying much attention, but little escapes the keen senses of the Sheepdog man. Old English Sheepdog men may seem like pussycats, and they can be, but they can also adopt a protective manner with those they love. They aren't overly aggressive like some breeds of men. But they won't run from a fight if push comes to shove. Although he takes his work seriously, when he has free time he knows how to have fun. Play is a Sheepdog man's favorite diversion, and he loves the outdoors. On the other hand, sometimes you have to lead him to exercise, but he'll feel better afterwards.

TRAINING: Training a Sheepdog man is not easy. It isn't because he lacks intelligence. In some areas, he is extremely intelligent. The challenge comes from his stubbornness. He can be independent, and if he decides he doesn't want to go to the opera, you may have to leave him at home and go with a friend or family member. The best way to train an Old English Sheepdog man is to start early, be consistent, be firm, and incorporate play into the training. When you show him what you want, reward him and make it fun. Then he'll want to play along. A Sheepdog man is sensitive, but he's also tough and forgiving. If you accidentally go ballistic, he'll not hold a grudge if you can drop it, move on, and have fun. Make sure your Sheepdog man gets plenty of exercise, and don't keep him cooped up inside for too long or he may become restless and bored.

SOCIAL SKILLS: Most people respect and like Sheepdog men because they are easy-going and friendly. Initially, they may be a little reserved with strangers, but, given time, they'll usually warm up to people. They are honest and forthright with people. Sheepdog men are not overly concerned about impressing people, but, in a family setting, they may be the opposite. These men are very concerned about how family and some close friends view them. They want very much to be loved and accepted by those they love and will go to great lengths to win approval. Because Sheepdog men are by nature herders, they may try to control people. Some do this physically, and others do it emotionally. With children, he can be a great caretaker. As the children grow older, he must learn to let them go their own way. In a relationship, these men are playful and extremely affectionate, sometimes more than a woman knows what to do with.

TYPE OF WOMAN: The woman for an Old English Sheepdog man will accept his herding nature. Once she discovers how he herds, physically or mentally, she must be sure she can accept it, because he'll never grow out of it. The playful Sheepdog man will require a woman who can be playful, even a bit silly at times. She'll recognize his stubborn streak and find ways to encourage him through play and reward to do what she asks. And, she'll allow him the freedom to occasionally dig his heels in and say "No."

TYPICAL OLD ENGLISH SHEEPDOG MAN: Jeff's story, as told by himself:

Standing in the middle of a street in Gainesville, Florida, my arms up to the sky, the words came desperate and urgent: "God, you put me on this earth, but for what?" Considering that I had lived for seven years as a devout atheist, something new had begun. Up to that moment, I held the belief that ideas of soul were security blankets people used to deal with death. Yeah, I was sure these physical bodies were bags of chemicals that had randomly come about over a long time. But this out loud, heartfelt acknowledgement that came strongly and without doubt was the end of a terrible suffering and the beginning of freedom.

I changed my life. For the first time ever, I found a spiritual path that had meaning for me. I had found a teacher whom I admired. I attended workshops, prayer groups, meditation seminars, anything that came my way. It was as if a light bulb that I didn't know existed inside myself suddenly turned on. After many years of following others, learning from others, and being in the presence of wise men and women, I was asked to lead. Me? What did I have to offer? Yes, I was always talking to people about my faith and my beliefs, encouraging them to follow, but to actually step into a position of leadership? I wasn't so sure about that. Not wanting to offend my teacher by refusing him, I said yes, hoping he knew what he was asking.

Despite my doubts, I easily stepped into the role, mainly because I never viewed myself as the leader. Rather, I saw us all as seekers, looking for meaning. My role was simply to share my experiences with the people under my care and be there for them in the way my teacher was for me. I was a gentle shepherd, looking over his flock, pointing the way, but not being pushy. One day, a woman came to me and asked, "How do you know God exists?"

"I don't," I replied. "But I don't know that He doesn't. Given a choice of believing He does or doesn't exist, I like living my life as if He does. For me, it makes life better. You have to decide what is best for you." She sat for a moment, eyes closed. Then she smiled, opened her eyes, and looked at me with tears of joy. "I like believing He's there too."

FAMOUS OLD ENGLISH SHEEPDOG MAN: John Lithgow as Dick Sullivan in *3rd Rock From the Sun*

Dick is large like an Old English Sheepdog with much poise and grace, but he also has an undercurrent of bumblingness that makes him adorable in a funny way. He makes an excellent commander in charge of a group of aliens sent to observe humans. On Earth, he pretends to be a teacher, and with both his alien group and his students, he is a bit controlling. Dick can be extremely stubborn, refusing to give in even when he knows it doesn't serve him. His girlfriend, Mary, trained him well, using reward and consistency.

6

THE SPORTING GROUP

THE SPORTING GROUP is made up of men who were designed to locate and retrieve items. They are generally easy to train and want very much to please those they love. They make good family men and are avid outdoorsmen.

AMERICAN COCKER SPANIEL: A long time ago, these guys could actually hunt. Now they're just cute, sweet companions.

BRITTANY: Outdoor ball sports are these spunky, multitalented guys' first passion. Second is being cuddled and petted.

GOLDEN RETRIEVER: These wonderful family men are fairly laid back and have such a love of ball sports that they could live with a ball attached to them and be very content.

IRISH SETTER: These sophisticated-looking but bouncy guys love to search for information. They may not do much with it, but they'll make it available to others.

LABRADOR RETRIEVER: He may never grow up, but this is Mr. All-American family man. Keep him busy, give him lots of exercise, and he'll be less destructive.

WEIMARANER: These guys are great sportsmen who love the outdoors. They tend to be more independent and stubborn than most of the sporting group men.

Qualities:

    Eager to please others

    Great companions

    Very sensitive

    Playful and everybody's friend

FINE FOR NOVICE WOMEN

Behavior with children:

Exercise required:

Activity level:

Ease of training:

Sociability with strangers:

Affection level:

Playfulness:

Protectiveness:

Watchdog ability:

PHYSICAL CHARACTERISTICS: The American Cocker Spaniel man can be very attractive in a slightly feminine way. They have pleading eyes that implore people to pay attention to them. Although they are in the sporting group, they typically prefer dressing up—more than the other sporting breeds. Appearance is very important to them, and they may spend more time in front of the mirror than your average guy.

ABILITIES & INTERESTS: Cocker Spaniel men are very curious and like to delve into things. While they are a sporting breed, they are exceptional in that they no longer have a strong hunting instinct. Instead, they prefer being a companion to others. They are so sweet, affectionate, playful, and willing to please that they can be proficient in any field requiring good people skills and an ability to follow orders. These men tend to be happy, even though their eyes may have a sad, pleading look to them. People who hang out with Cocker Spaniel men find it almost impossible to be unhappy. They're like a beam of sunshine. These men enjoy some athletic activities. Ball sports are fun, although they rarely pursue sports with the attention that some of the other breeds like the Golden and Labrador Retriever men do. They prefer sports where they can be with others. Jogging by themselves is less fun than with a partner.

TRAINING: A Cocker Spaniel man is easy to train because he wants so much to please. He will often second-guess what someone wants and do it before being asked. This much attentiveness might be excessive for some women; other women will eagerly receive it. A few words of praise to let a Cocker Spaniel man know when he's done a good job are usually enough. He will appreciate rewards as well, but they're not necessary. Scolding him or yelling at him will only hurt him. He's just too sweet to deserve this type of treatment. It's best to ignore unwanted behavior and encourage the good. He will respond quickly. There are a few Cocker Spaniel men who have been taken advantage of and abused. These men tend to be more scared and may snap or become rebellious. Sometimes there is nothing that can be done to change this behavior, but some, given a lot of love, patience, and consistency, can open up and become happy, trusting Cocker Spaniel men.

SOCIAL SKILLS: Cocker Spaniel men love the company of others. They are completely at ease with people, even upon first encounters. Most people find these men easy to be around. People will often reveal their whole life stories to these men, because Cocker Spaniel men are such great listeners. They like having lots of friends and these friendships can run very deep. Their friendships often go back to high school. If anyone ever needs them, they are ready to help out. At work, they excel at following orders and usually get things done on time, although their desire to visit with others will sometimes slow them down. Children love Cocker Spaniel men for their gentle, playful, loving natures. These men can be frisky and silly at times, making children squeal with delight. They tend to be doting fathers. In a relationship, they are extremely affectionate and will want to spend time with their partners. Life with a Cocker Spaniel man is easy if a woman enjoys constant companionship and a man who will do anything she asks.

TYPE OF WOMAN: The best woman for a Cocker Spaniel man enjoys a companion who wants very much to be with her and please her. She'll be playful. Family will be important to her, and she will want to have children. She'll understand his gregarious nature and want to attend social functions with him. She'll have an even temper and realize there is no need to be harsh with this man.

TYPICAL AMERICAN COCKER SPANIEL MAN: Luke's story, as told by his older sister, Tabitha:

Luke was always extra-sensitive, and he tried to make everyone happy. In a way, that made him the black sheep of the family.

Christmas, 1986, we all convened at the annual family get-together. That included Mom, Dad, Luke, our other brother Rex and me, Tabitha. Luke had read this book by John Bradshaw about families, and he was excited to point out the dysfunctional aspects of our family. Maybe it would be different now, but at that time, none of us was ready to hear it. Mom and Dad's only form of communication was yelling at each other. Rex got into drugs, and I escaped via alcohol. So Luke was right, only we were all in denial. We were living in our fantasy worlds and couldn't hear him.

It took me five years to finally understand what he was talking about. That's when I started going to Alcoholics Anonymous and went sober. Twelve years later, I'm still sober. The rest of the family didn't change anything, but Luke and I still had hope.

Last year, Luke called from the hospital. He had cancer and the doctors didn't give him long to live. I stayed with him the last weeks of his life. A couple of days before he died he said, "I don't mind dying young, I just wish I had accomplished more."

"Luke," I said, "Honey, you changed my life. It was your voice I heard inside myself telling me to go sober for five years. If I hadn't had that, nothing would have changed."

He smiled. "I am grateful for that, Tabitha. I just wish I could have helped Mom and Dad also."

At the funeral, hundreds of people showed up, which surprised me and my family. All these complete strangers came up to us, crying, saying how Luke had changed their lives. They talked about how his compassion and love helped them make it through tough times and how selflessly he gave of his time to support them! I was stunned! Obviously, Luke had done more with his life than we knew. That he wanted to have done more amazed me. It wasn't long after that that his final wish came true. My parents started taking dance lessons together, and their relationship has improved. I wish it hadn't taken his death to make a difference for them, but wherever Luke is, I'm sure he's smiling.

FAMOUS COCKER SPANIEL MAN: Nathan Lane as Albert Goldman in *The Birdcage*

Albert plays the soft, feminine side of the relationship with his partner, Armand, in the more masculine role. It doesn't take much to upset Albert, since he's so sensitive. At the beginning of the movie when he thinks Armand is having an affair, Albert cries and laments that he's gotten older and gained weight. Gregarious and outgoing, he makes the rounds to all the shops, visiting with everyone he meets. His relationship with Val, Armand's son, is filled with nurturing and loving qualities.

QUALITIES:

- MULTITALENTED
- EAGER TO PLEASE
- LOVE OUTDOOR SPORTS
- SELECTIVE IN THEIR FRIENDSHIPS

FINE FOR NOVICE WOMEN

Behavior with children:

Exercise required:

Activity level:

Ease of training:

Sociability with strangers:

Affection level:

Playfulness:

Protectiveness:

Watchdog ability:

PHYSICAL CHARACTERISTICS: The Brittany man is less imposing than some of the sporting men. This may be due to a smaller size or it may be his demeanor. They can blend in well with their surroundings and go unnoticed when they want. Casual, sporty dress is their favorite.

ABILITIES & INTERESTS: Brittany men are multitalented, a combination of other sporting men rolled into one. Like the Irish Setter, they are capable of searching in a methodical way for information, people, whatever. Once they have found what they are looking for they will let others know and then, if asked, bring it back. Most other sporting men will look for it, find it, or retrieve it, but not all three. Usually Brittany men prefer being outdoors, especially if they grew up camping, hiking, or playing sports outdoors. They enjoy ball sports and will probably play, coach, or watch sports most of their lives. While they can live in the city, most Brittany men love having extra room to play and let loose. They are experts in playfulness. Exercise is a must for these men every day or they become restless and destructive. These men work well with others and take instruction very well because they have a strong desire to please others.

TRAINING: Training a Brittany man is easy because he is so devoted and eager to please. He will often assist someone before being asked. For independent women, this may be too much. For women who like complete attention and obedience, he is awesome. A few words of praise given to a Brittany man will get you almost anything you ask for. If you are verbally harsh with him, he can become completely despondent or almost annoying trying to make up for any misdeed, whether it was his fault or not. There is really no need to belittle him because he tries so hard. Instead, you can be more clear with what you would like and encourage him by letting him know how much you believe in him.

SOCIAL SKILLS:
Brittany men can be a bit standoffish when they first meet someone. Most of the time they are just shy and uncomfortable when meeting new people. Once they know someone and like him, they can be very playful and become loyal friends. They may not have a large circle of friends, but they are very devoted to those they connect with. Their friendships tend to revolve around quality, not quantity. Brittany men are excellent with children. Being very playful puts these men at the top of most children's lists of favorite adults. As fathers, they are fantastic, being very patient, gentle, and loving. In a relationship, these men are very devoted and will worship the ground a woman walks on if she lets him. He wants so hard to please and will do anything he can to make a woman happy.

TYPE OF WOMAN:
The woman for a Brittany will appreciate his strong desire to please her and will not be put off by his constant attention. She will enjoy physical activity, playing, and being outdoors. Children will be important to her, because he will probably want to be a father. She will understand his need to be a searcher and give him praise for a job well done.

TYPICAL BRITTANY MAN:
Tom's story, as told by his wife, Laura:

Tom and I are in our early thirties and have not yet had children. But we seem to be magnets for the four girls ranging in age six to fifteen who live down the street. One Sunday afternoon, they asked their mother if they could ride their bikes over to Laura and Tom's house. Their mother thought for a moment, confused because she couldn't think of any of their friends in the neighborhood named Laura or Tom. Finally they got the point across to her that we were the Laura and Tom they wanted to visit. She laughed and sent them over to our house.

Well, I am one of those people who can get very focused on a task and not want to stop until it is done. On this afternoon, I was in the middle of attempting to organize our study when the girls showed up. I reluctantly put my project on the back shelf and we first played their favorite game, backgammon. After about three games, rampant cheating began to surface on the ten-year-old girl's side. They got bored with backgammon.

Immediately the six-year-old utters, "So, what do you want to do now?"

Organize our study. But of course, I said, "How about we go play in the backyard?"

We played in the backyard, played pool on the pool table, and ate a snack. During the snack, my husband wandered in from the garage. He had heard at least two of three "So, what do you want to do now?" phrases throughout the afternoon. On this last one, he saw my expression and immediately sent me back to the study and got the kids some more juice to drink. About 20 minutes later, I noticed that the house was totally quiet. Intrigued, I went looking for everyone. When I opened the garage door, the scene before me made me realize that Tom is more than an amazing husband.

He also has some kind of superhuman powers when it comes to children. The girls had neatly placed Tom's baseball and golf equipment on a shelf. The six-year-old had the shop-vac running on one side of the garage, while the ten-year-old was being taught what I would call the "How To Use a Blower to Clean the Garage, Intermediate Course." I laughed hysterically for a full minute. Not only had my husband rescued me when I was in need, without a word from me or even the slightest hint of bother from him, but he had found a way to get someone else's children to help him clean our garage and have fun doing it.

FAMOUS BRITTANY MAN: Chris Rock as Lance Burton in *Down To Earth*

Chris knows what he wants and goes after it. He's clever, determined, and talented. Disgruntled by losing his body and being temporarily placed in another body, he makes the best of it. As a comedian, he takes life events, twists them around until they are funny, and then takes them to his audience. When he meets Sontee, he will do anything to make her happy, including giving back to the community.

QUALITIES:

EAGER TO PLEASE OTHERS
EVERYBODY'S FRIEND
SPORTS-ORIENTED
ALL-AROUND "GREAT GUY"

FINE FOR NOVICE WOMEN

Behavior with children:

Exercise required:

Activity level:

Ease of training:

Sociability with strangers:

Affection level:

Playfulness:

Protectiveness:

Watchdog ability:

PHYSICAL CHARACTERISTICS: Golden Retriever men are usually lean and physically fit. They love to spend time outdoors, and it shows. They are similar to Labrador Retriever men, but what distinguishes them is their hair tends to be longer and their faces are leaner. Because they love sports, they are often dressed for baseball, soccer, or some other sport. They are very attentive to the clothes they wear. Most of the time, they prefer casual dress but look excellent dressed up.

ABILITIES & INTERESTS: Golden Retriever men are excellent at retrieving information and bringing it back to others. Their presentation style is very gentle, and while they can be very generous in sharing what they know, they can also be very competitive. Their strong work ethic and desire to please others, including those they work for, will oftentimes keep them at the office until late. But they also enjoy quiet time where they can kick back and relax, and it is important that they find time for themselves. Golden Retriever men also love sports and as adults will continue to play, coach, or watch sports. Their favorite sports usually involve a ball.

TRAINING: Training a Golden Retriever man is easy because he is intelligent and has such a strong desire to please. He will often do what is expected of him without being asked, which sounds great, but there are some women who become annoyed by his eagerness to please. One challenge is whether or not he has the time to do everything on a woman's list. Because he is so busy with work, sports, and spending time with friends, he has a tendency to spread himself thin. A Golden Retriever man is very easygoing and can put up with some harsh words. But he is such a sweetheart he really needs to be loved and appreciated. Praise will work wonders in getting a Golden to do what you want.

SOCIAL SKILLS: Golden Retriever men are extremely social and outgoing. They tend to have many friends, and spending quality time with their friends is important. It is common for them to have friendships going back to high school days. At work, they get along well with others and are excellent team players. Strangers immediately like Golden men and find them easy to talk to. They are the kind of men most people trust, and the more a new acquaintance gets to know a Golden man, the more this trust grows. Family is very important to Golden Retriever men. This includes their extended family, mom, dad, brothers, and sisters. Most Golden men will want a family of their own. Since they are such excellent fathers, this is a good thing. A Golden Retriever man will try everything in his power to make the woman in his life happy. She can expect extreme amounts of affection.

TYPE OF WOMAN: The best woman for a Golden Retriever will appreciate his love of family and sports. She'll enjoy spending time outdoors with him. Because he is so busy with work, sports, and friends, she may have to get creative in having quality time with him. She'll appreciate his strong desire to please her and others.

TYPICAL GOLDEN RETRIEVER MAN: Jim's story, as told by his ex-girlfriend, Jessica:

High school, senior year, a time of magic because I had my first taste of love. Not my first boyfriend, but the first boy I knew I loved and who loved me back equally. He adored me, and I couldn't get enough. He treated me like a lady—opening the door of his MG convertible every time; calling me every night to tell me he loved me; holding my hand at the movies as if it were a precious, fragile rose petal. And if ever I asked for something, he went out of his way to get it. Watching him with his mother told me "this guy's for real." He also cherished her and eagerly helped her, even before she asked.

One summer day, he told me this girl, Kim, had asked him to the Scorpions concert. Jim and I could spend hours listening to their music. We had all their lyrics committed to memory. Excitedly I said, "Awesome, you'll have the best time."

He looked at me puzzled. "You don't mind if I go?"

Well, of course I didn't because I knew I could trust him. Besides, it was a chance to see the Scorpions!

After the concert he called me and said they were great. But it wasn't until later that I got the whole story, and even then it came from a friend, not him. My next-door neighbor, Andrea, also went to the concert, unbeknownst to Jim and me. Out of thousands of concertgoers whom should she bump in to at the entrance but my sweetheart, Jim, and Kim. So they all sat on the grass next to each other. Throughout the concert Jim kept saying, "Jessica would love this." Or "This is Jessica's favorite part coming up here!" By the end of the concert Kim's jaw was clenched, as were her punch-ready fists. Andrea said Jim was clueless. He was too busy enjoying the music to notice Kim's response to his comments. Kim never asked Jim out again.

Separate colleges eventually took their toll on our relationship, and we split, although we ended things amicably. Years later, after dating other more challenging breeds, I can better appreciate the easy, eager-to-please attitude of a Golden Retriever. I hope women in relationships with Golden Retriever men realize how blessed they are.

FAMOUS GOLDEN RETRIEVER MAN: Brad Pitt as the young man in the coffee shop in *Meet Joe Black*

When Brad Pitt first enters the movie, he is a young, friendly, charismatic guy. Family is obviously important because he starts the scene on the phone giving loving advice to his sister. Relaxed and outgoing, he easily starts up a conversation with a complete stranger as if they were long-time friends. He talks about wanting to please a woman and being willing to do whatever it takes to make a woman happy. Later in the movie, when another personality, Joe Black, enters his body, he becomes a Doberman Pinscher.

THE IRISH SETTER MAN

QUALITIES:

> REFINED, UPSTANDING GENTLEMAN
>
> PLAYFUL, EVEN CLOWNISH
>
> LOYAL AND DEVOTED
>
> GREAT FAMILY MAN

FINE FOR NOVICE WOMEN

Behavior with children:

Exercise required:

Activity level:

Ease of training:

Sociability with strangers:

Affection level:

Playfulness:

Protectiveness:

Watchdog ability:

PHYSICAL CHARACTERISTICS: Irish Setter men often present themselves as distinguished gentlemen, but it doesn't take long for people to pick up on their somewhat clownish side. These men are particular about their appearance. They try to achieve a certain sophisticated look while dressing in casual, sporty attire.

ABILITIES & INTERESTS: Setter men have a talent for covering an area, finding what is hidden, and revealing it to others. In a work environment, they make great team players because they enjoy the company of others. It may take them longer to accomplish a task due to their socializing with co-workers. They are capable of hard work although most prefer to be men of leisure. Whether or not they are men of leisure, they will keep busy with projects, going a mile a minute. Setters often like to be the center of attention and can play the role of clown when sophistication doesn't get them the attention they seek. All Setters enjoy physical exercise: running, biking, swimming, and athletic sports.

TRAINING: An Irish Setter man wants very much to please and, most of the time, he is very agreeable to doing as asked. Some people think he is lacking in brain power—not so. He can, however, be easily distracted. If he does not respond immediately, have some patience and use lots of praise to get his attention. Consistency and firm resolve also assist in training a Setter man. Incorporating play into a request is very effective.

SOCIAL SKILLS: Irish Setter men make friends easily and usually have a large network of friends. The paradox with Setter men is that they love people and are very social and at the same time enjoy their independence. These men are very devoted family men. Children are sometimes uncertain when they first meet an Irish Setter man, but they soon warm up to him because they see in him a childlike spirit and a genuine appreciation for children. In relationships, Irish Setter men are extremely loyal and devoted. They can be very affectionate, almost too much for some women.

TYPE OF WOMAN: The woman for an Irish Setter will appreciate his occasional need for independence, his desire to please, and his need for friends and companionship. He'll need consistency and firmness from her, along with lots of praise. She must be prepared for his possible split personality. One minute he may be very serious and upright, and the next he may be silly, even childish. She'll be understanding, even amused if he acts like the fool during a party.

TYPICAL IRISH SETTER MAN: Miles' story, as told by his wife, Carrie:

I had a crush on one man but fell in love with another. The twist? It was the same man. When I first met Miles, he seemed so elegant, charming, and witty. When he walked into the room, I didn't notice him immediately, but that didn't last long. He started telling a story about a trip he took from New York to California, by motorcycle, in 1969. He painted a colorful story, describing the way people's clothing styles changed. "In New York we were high style—slick. Black, white, silver, and some bright colors. By the time I reached California, I was in the land of psychedelic Oz colors. My head spun from so much retinal stimulation." He was so vibrant, happy and alive—I was very taken with him.

Miles and I talked some that night and, before leaving, he asked for my number. He called the next day, and we made plans to go out the following weekend. *A Room With a View* was showing at the time. Even today, I still wonder if his plan included a soft love story just so he could seduce me. He refuses to confess. Anyway, it worked, my heart was open, and I was even more attracted to him. I didn't fall in love with him at that point, though. That was yet to come.

We dated for two months and I really liked Miles, but I wasn't sure he was the one. Then one night, it happened. Miles was speaking in front of the Toastmasters group we belonged to. Although he was mostly bald on the top of his head, Miles would comb the hair from the left side across the top to cover up the bald spot. Somehow his "comb-over hair" got messed up, and it was sticking straight up. Looking around the room I noticed everyone was suppressing a laugh. It wasn't just the comb-over; it was that Miles carried himself as such a gentleman, and this flop with his hair made him more real, more human, more fun. It was in that moment that I fell in love with him. Over the years, I've realized there is a silly, playful side to Miles. Sometimes he's trying to be funny, but oftentimes he's just funny without trying, and that's when I love him the most.

FAMOUS IRISH SETTER MAN: Ralph Fiennes as Count Laszlo Almasy in *The English Patient*

Count Laszlo is an Irish Setter who is dignified and reserved. In *The English Patient*, the Count has the Irish Setter's setting instinct, traversing uncharted areas to bring back maps of various regions. He's independent, but once he falls in love with Katherine, he practically demands constant companionship from her. After she lets him in a little, he keeps after her, even when she says no.

QUALITIES:

INTEREST IN SPORTS

DESIRE TO PLEASE THE WOMAN IN HIS LIFE

FAMILY VALUES

MAKE-THINGS-HAPPEN ATTITUDE

FINE FOR NOVICE WOMEN

Behavior with children:

Exercise required:

Activity level:

Ease of training:

Sociability with strangers:

Affection level:

Playfulness:

Protectiveness:

Watchdog ability:

PHYSICAL CHARACTERISTICS: Labrador Retriever men are athletic and ruggedly handsome with strong jaw lines. They prefer to wear their hair short as opposed to the Golden Retriever, who has longer locks. They make excellent eye contact and have great smiles.

ABILITIES & INTERESTS: Labrador men are retrievers, and they enjoy doing things for others. Tireless in their pursuits, they can run errands, make sales calls, perform surgery, and keep going as long as they feel appreciated. Labrador men excel in any profession where people skills are a plus. People tend to trust Labrador men because they are caring, compassionate men with strong ethical values. They have an "All-American" kind of charm about them and people respond to that. Labrador men enjoy working and have strong work ethics. Labradors are sports enthusiasts. They especially love ball sports and will continue this passion as they grow older through playing, coaching, watching games, collecting cards, etc.

TRAINING: Training a Labrador man is very easy, because he wants so much to please those he loves. As long as you are clear in your communication, he will do everything in his power to accommodate you. A Labrador man can handle some harsh treatment. However, he is such a sweet man, I strongly encourage you to use positive feedback instead. If you do this he will absolutely treat you like a queen. The only challenge you might have is his destructive tendencies when bored. This usually takes the form of projects that get out of hand and appear to never end. Let him stay busy with activities he enjoys.

SOCIAL SKILLS: Most people are immediately at ease with Labrador men. These men are extremely social. Oftentimes they still have friends from high school. At work they are always willing to help out, and they enjoy working on projects with others. They follow instructions well. Family, both immediate and extended, is very important to the Labrador man. It is fortunate when a woman likes his family, because she will be spending time with them. Lots of time. As a father, he is awesome. He can be firm and yet extremely loving, devoted, and very playful. In a relationship, a Lab man will be very loyal and affectionate. He'll want to stay close by a woman's side, except when he's busy working or spending time with friends.

TYPE OF WOMAN: The woman most suited for a Labrador man will love the outdoors and sports. She will enjoy spending time with her man close at her side except when he is working, and then she'll understand his consuming commitment to work. She'll understand his gregarious nature and realize that he'll want to spend time with friends and family.

TYPICAL LABRADOR RETRIEVER MAN: John's story, as told by himself:

We had been friends since the seventh grade and, even though I don't remember exactly when I first met her, I know it must have been on the first or second day of school. You see, we both played trombone in the middle school band, and I was new to this school. She was first chair, and I was second. This would prove to be the pattern for the next five years as we made our way through grades 8–12. During this time, we were great friends with the same circle of friends. We never dated, but we did go on a couple of double dates.

It was during our second year in college that it happened. We had our first date! This was a little awkward because, up to this point, our relationship had been more like brother and sister. Even though we attended separate colleges, we continued to date during our sophomore, junior, and senior years. Early in our relationship, while she was giving me a tour of her college, she told me a story of how her dad proposed to her mother near a certain tree and park bench on campus. I filed this information away, not knowing if it would ever be useful.

By the time our senior year arrived, we were in dating bliss, and I knew this was the girl for me. Recalling the story she told me, I knew a similar proposal would be impossible to beat. I was ready to make it all happen—if I only had a ring. Being a poor college kid, the only asset I possessed was a collection of baseball cards. Spring break arrived, and I was going to be in a couple of large cities which would each have a number of dealers who might be interested in my cards.

I was stunned! No one was in the market to buy baseball cards. Nada, nope, zip! I returned to my small college town rejected. Within a day or two, though, I heard of a local baseball card dealer who had just opened a new store. I drove to see him and after a few minutes he purchased some of my best cards: a 1939 Joe DiMaggio, a 1954 Al Kaline rookie, a 1968 Johnny Bench rookie, and a 1972 complete set. Even though I knew the baseball cards would continue to appreciate in value, I knew my relationship with the woman I loved would appreciate many times more.

That day, with money in hand, I drove 350 miles round-trip to purchase the ring that I knew she would love. Everything had happened so fast, but there was time for one more trip. I drove 90 miles to her college and told her that I was just passing through town. I said we had enough time to share a meal. We had dinner at a nice restaurant and then went back to campus to take a stroll. When we arrived at the spot where her father had proposed to her mother, I got down on one knee and asked her to marry me. She immediately said yes—but did not think I had a ring to give her. When I pulled out the ring, she was quite shocked and elated. She said, "Yes!" Everything had gone perfectly.

FAMOUS LABRADOR RETRIEVER MAN: Matthew Perry as Chandler on *Friends*

Chandler is eager to please, sometimes to the point of going overboard. Like the time he got on his knees and proposed to Monica or, later, when he took wedding photos of another wedding because he lost all the disposable cameras that Monica had set on the tables at their wedding. He's everyone's best friend—your typical, all-around great guy. He loves ball sports, is often seen playing foosball, or tossing a ball around with his roommate, Joey. And there are several episodes where Chandler and Joey excitedly discuss going to see a basketball game.

QUALITIES:

LOVE OF THE HUNT
INDEPENDENT
BOLD AND COURAGEOUS
ACTIVE, BUSY LIFESTYLE

FOR EXPERIENCED WOMEN DUE TO: INDEPENDENCE AND STUBBORNNESS

Behavior with children: 🦴 🦴

Exercise required: 🦴 🦴 🦴

Activity level: 🦴 🦴 🦴

Ease of training: 🦴

Sociability with strangers: 🦴 🦴

Affection level: 🦴 🦴

Playfulness: 🦴 🦴 🦴

Protectiveness: 🦴 🦴 🦴

Watchdog ability: 🦴 🦴 🦴

PHYSICAL CHARACTERISTICS: Weimaraner men are athletic and physically fit. They have mysterious, steely eyes that seem like empty, bottomless pits. Because they love the outdoors, they prefer a sporty, casual dress that reflects this lifestyle. These men are particular about their appearance and stay neatly groomed.

ABILITIES & INTERESTS: These men excel at hunting and can take on large projects. They can be extremely focused and determined. Compared to the other sporting breeds of men, the Weimaraner is very independent and will think for himself. In the field this can be a plus, especially if he is self-employed or works for someone who trusts him and will let him do what he has to do. All the sporting breeds of men need exercise, but, with a Weimaraner man, that need may be quadrupled. He absolutely has to have exercise and will need lots of it. He also has the tendency to go a mile a minute and never stop. A Weimaraner man may not understand why everyone else can't keep up with him, and he can be a hard, disciplined taskmaster. He doesn't ask more of someone than he himself will give, but not everyone is able to focus and have the amount of energy he does. Weimaraner men love the outdoors, and they love to play. They are at their best when living in the country, doing something outside on a frequent basis. These men also tend to be more protective than the other sporting breeds of men.

TRAINING: Training a Weimaraner man can be very challenging. He is very independent and headstrong. If he respects someone, and the person knows how to approach him, he can be somewhat obedient. However, it will still take an infinite amount of patience and consistency to train him. Another challenge is the Weimaraner man's high need for exercise and always-on-the-go activity level. If he's busy and focused, he may not pay attention to anyone or anything else. Training him requires a lot of praise and rewards. Criticism and harshness tend to roll off him, but too much can lead to attitude problems later on. An independent woman who can get things done herself will find him easier to be in a relationship with, especially if she doesn't need him to respond immediately or at all to her request.

SOCIAL SKILLS: Weimaraner men can be friendly when they want to be, but they are very selective about whom they open up to. Usually they have buddies who they spend time with, especially guys that they hunt, work, or exercise with. Even within this group of friends, there are only a few that the Weimaraner will reveal himself to. He can be very private. They also find it challenging to find friends and family who can keep up with them. This is important to a Weimaraner man. These men can be wonderful fathers in that they are loving, giving, and excellent role models for discipline and hard work. Infants are not their strong suit, but as children grow older, the Weimaraners are more equipped to handle them. They can be protective of their families if need be. In a relationship, these men can be affectionate and playful. When they truly love someone, they are very loyal. Their high degree of independence and activity will have some women feeling alone and abandoned, but there are women who would welcome this.

TYPE OF WOMAN: The woman for a Weimaraner man will honor his independence and his high level of competence. She will recognize his need for exercise and activity and let him stay as busy as he wants to be. Her happiness will not depend on his level of obedience. She can take care of herself. The partner for a Weimaraner man needs to be playful, and an appreciation of the outdoors would be a plus.

Typical Weimaraner Man: Chuck's story, as told by his cousin, Rose:

Chuck, having grown up in a rural area outside of Austin, Texas, knew how to hunt and how to watch out for snakes. If a rattlesnake crossed his path, he wouldn't hesitate to kill it in the interest of general safety. When he moved to Freer, Texas, he began serious rattlesnake hunting for the Texas Rattlesnake Roundup. For years he caught and killed hundreds of snakes. On one occasion, he had a sack full of snakes in the back of his pickup. One got loose, and as Chuck looked behind him, the snake struck at him and hit the window. Unaffected, he got out and put the snake back in the sack.

A few years ago, he took me arrowhead hunting and, while we were out, he also looked for rattlesnakes. Despite being out all day searching every crevice, looking under every rock and into every hiding place that snakes like, Chuck didn't find one snake. On the drive home, there in the road stretched a six-foot rattlesnake.

Chuck stopped the car and just watched that snake slowly move across the road. I looked at Chuck, expecting him to drive over the snake. But he just watched the snake, and after it left he said, "You know, Rose, I never saw one snake today. Unless someone is in danger, I don't think I can kill any more snakes. If we don't stop killing them, they'll all be gone."

I had always appreciated my cousin Chuck, and at that moment I appreciated him more than ever. Because I realized that Chuck valued the life of a snake and would even go so far as to shift his behavior in order to preserve rattlesnakes in Texas.

Famous Weimaraner Man: George Clooney as Everett Ulysses McGill in *O' Brother, Where Art Thou*

Everett and his two buddies wander the countryside on a quest. Independent, active, self-assured, and driven define Everett. He works well with his friends, but he can take care of himself. Regardless of the difficulties they encounter, he doesn't give up. He may not be the best husband or father, seeing as how he leaves his family, but his ultimate desire is to make life better for them and for himself. When he finds his wife and children with another man, the protective side comes out and he punches the guy.

7

THE HOUND GROUP

THE HOUND GROUP of men have a strong desire to hunt, whether for information, women, animals, or something else. Accustomed to hunting alone or with other men, they can be very independent and stubborn.

BASSET HOUND: Despite their somewhat sad, hang-dog look, these loveable men have great hearts and wonderful, sweet dispositions.

BEAGLE: What fun, busy family men these guys can be. Having been given an incredible sniffer, they can chase down anything.

BLOODHOUND: Tracking is a passion for these guys. Just turn them loose and they can sniff out and find anything. In their time off, they prefer to rest.

BORZOI: These sighthounds hunt by sight, and if they see something they want, they're off. Like cats, they are sensitive, independent, stubborn and affectionate . . . on their terms.

DACHSHUND: These stubborn but sweet guys love to dig up dirt. Sometimes it's information, or it could be gardening.

NORWEGIAN ELKHOUND: These affectionate men love to hunt, and they'll let everyone know when they're hot on the trail. Multitalented, these men are capable of hunting, guarding, pulling, and many other service-oriented tasks.

RHODESIAN RIDGEBACK: Unique among the hound men because they use multiple senses to hunt, and they are very protective. These men are fearless and tough.

QUALITIES:

FOCUSED DETECTIVE (SEARCHER)

LIKES TO TAKE LIFE EASY

MOVES AT HIS OWN PACE

HIS TALKING CAN SOUND LIKE "BAYING"

FINE FOR NOVICE WOMEN

Behavior with children:

Exercise required:

Activity level:

Ease of training:

Sociability with strangers:

Affection level:

Playfulness:

Protectiveness:

Watchdog ability:

PHYSICAL CHARACTERISTICS: Basset Hound men may have a slightly sad look about them, perhaps because they had a difficult past. Regardless of their history, they tend to be happy men. They are sturdy, laid-back men who are most comfortable in casual attire. If they do get dressed up, they'll loosen their ties the first chance they get.

ABILITIES & INTERESTS: A Basset Hound man loves to track. It may be people, information, etc. Once on the trail, he's extremely hard to shake off. Generally, he prefers to pursue activities that require little physical exertion. He tends to move at a slower pace than some other breeds, but he is persistent, and his slower speed can make it easier for others to follow him. He can work well with others or by himself. Basset Hound men can make great orators because they have deep voices and like to hear themselves howl. Most Basset Hound men like some form of exercise that doesn't require speed, such as walking, lifting weights, etc.

TRAINING: Training a Basset Hound man is only slightly challenging. Much of it will depend on your attitude and consistency. He can be stubborn and have a one-track mind when he's hot on a trail. Scolding, nagging, and yelling rarely work. He'll just look abused and may go off in a sulk. Praise and good food will win him over most of the time. As long as you do not expect immediate results when you ask him to do something, you'll be much happier. He can be hard to housebreak (cleanliness and picking up after himself are not major concerns of his).

SOCIAL SKILLS: The Basset Hound man is genuinely a great guy. He's easy to get along with, and most people find him pleasant. Even if he holds back when first meeting strangers, they immediately feel at ease with him. Co-workers enjoy the Basset Hound man and admire his ability to stick with a project. At home, the Basset man is loving, devoted, giving, and fairly even-tempered. Children love him and enjoy playing rough–and-tumble games with him. In a relationship, he enjoys companionship and, at the same time, he can be somewhat independent and take care of himself. He appreciates affection and will return it when he's in the mood.

TYPE OF WOMAN: The woman for a Basset man will appreciate and not take advantage of his sweet nature. She'll understand that he may become preoccupied when he's on the trail and that he may even forget her or previous engagements they may have planned. If he becomes stubborn, she'll find ways to coax him instead of pushing or pulling. She may have to accept his inability to pick up after himself.

TYPICAL BASSET HOUND MAN: Arno's story, as told by his wife, Belinda:

I hear women in their 30s lamenting the fact that they're single. Desperate to find a man, they'll go anywhere, try anything. I just chuckle because I know love has its own timing. When my husband of many years and I divorced, I had no need for a relationship, so I decided to go back to school. At age 65, I became a doctor. Life was good. I traveled and worked with people in many other countries.

One night, at a meeting of the cultural exchange group that I'm a member of, I met a man from Germany who had been born in Poland. I was born in Germany but grew up in Holland, so we had some things in common. We also had an attraction for each other, and, being a hound man, Arno started pursuing me. He would make trips from Germany to the States to spend weeks with me. Then he started inviting me to Germany and suggested we take trips together to see other places. I was tickled. Here, at age 69, I was being courted by a 70-year-old man!

After many trips, Arno told me in a phone conversation that his daughter had asked if we were getting married and he said he had told her "yes." Well, I thought! This is news to me! He hasn't asked me to marry him! But I didn't say anything. Then, when I went to visit him in Germany, he said, "We should go buy our wedding rings." Again, I didn't say anything but I thought it funny that he still had not asked. I loved him and would happily marry him—I just thought he would ask at some point.

Months later, we were in Germany at German happy hour with many of his friends. Arno stood up and, in his Basset Hound manner, bayed, "I have an announcement to make. After fifteen months and seven trips to see Belinda in the States, we're getting married." Everyone congratulated us, and I'm thinking he still hasn't asked me. Later that evening, a friend of his said, "So, Arno, it took you seven tries to find the courage to ask her to marry you."

Oh, thought Arno, I never asked her. So there at the party, Arno came up behind me and put his arms around me. He whispered in my ear, "Belinda, I've never asked you to marry me. Will you marry me?" Finally. I smiled, "Yes, Arno. I'll marry you."

FAMOUS BASSET HOUND MAN: David Schwimmer as Ross on *Friends*

Ross has that hang-dog look, with those sad Basset eyes. His voice has a deep baying sound. He's a kind, sensitive companion. Sometimes, when he is hot on the trail, it takes some effort to get his attention, as in the episode where he discovers that students are making out in the corner of the library where his published paleontology book is placed. When whining to the librarian doesn't work, Ross makes it his mission to catch lovers who dare to make out in front of his book.

QUALITIES:

    PLAYFUL FAMILY MAN

    EASY-TO-FOLLOW HOUND MAN

    GROUP-ORIENTED

    VOCAL WHEN EXCITED

FINE FOR NOVICE WOMEN

Behavior with children:	🦴 🦴 🦴
Exercise required:	🦴 🦴
Activity level:	🦴 🦴 🦴
Ease of training:	🦴 🦴
Sociability with strangers:	🦴 🦴 🦴
Affection level:	🦴 🦴 🦴
Playfulness:	🦴 🦴
Protectiveness:	🦴
Watchdog ability:	🦴 🦴

PHYSICAL CHARACTERISTICS: Beagle men are dapper-looking fellows. They are fun-loving, cheerful men who often have a smile on their face. People immediately trust these men because they have such a charming, friendly look to them. While they can dress up and look nice, they prefer casual, sporty attire. They spend little time on their appearance. Too many things to do, places to go, and people to see.

ABILITIES & INTERESTS: Beagle men enjoy the hunt. Each Beagle man may pursue a different place, person, or thing. But regardless of their quarry, when they are hot on the trail they all enjoy the companionship of others. They work great as team players and truly seem to have fun, whatever the task, especially when they have others around them. At the same time, they can be independent and think for themselves. They are also excellent problem solvers. Beagle men have a great sense of humor and a comical side that makes them fun and easy to be around. They can be vocal and verbose, entertaining people with their stories for hours on end. Real go-getters, these men like to stay busy and can accomplish a great deal when they set their minds to it. Exercise is important for Beagle men, because they love to eat. This is where their noses can get them into trouble. If they stay busy and get enough exercise, it is not a problem, but a sedentary Beagle man will tend to have weight issues. Sports activities involving others appeal to them the most, even if it's just jogging with a friend. If a Beagle man has trouble exercising, find him a partner.

TRAINING: A Beagle man wants to please, and he pays attention most of the time. Challenges occur when he is in pursuit, although it is easier to get his attention than some of the other hound dog men. Being independent, he sometimes thinks he has a better solution. Keep in mind that he is only trying to help. Praise works well as does reward, just don't use too much food as a reward due to his potential weight problem. The best way to train the Beagle man is with play and group activities. He wants to be a part of what everyone else is doing and he despises being left out. He can be sensitive, so be careful about harsh criticism. Although he will shake off criticism, he's so sweet and would never think of hurting anyone—why hurt him? Housebreaking can be a challenge, as picking up after himself may not be a priority. Usually he will get better with time.

SOCIAL SKILLS: Beagle men immediately put everyone at ease. They are genuine, sweet, fun, entertaining men. They tend to have many friends and enjoy the company of others. It doesn't always matter what they are doing; the important thing is having fun in the company of people they enjoy. In a work environment, they are team players and look to others for support. They can also work independently when need be. These men are awesome with children. They absolutely love and adore children, perhaps because they can be so childlike themselves. Most Beagle men will want to have children and will be very devoted to every aspect of their child's life. In a relationship, Beagle men are extremely affectionate and will have a strong desire to spend a lot of time with their partners. Being independent and hound dogs, they will sometimes take off and give chase, but they move a bit slower than other hound men, making it easier to keep an eye on them.

TYPE OF WOMAN: The best woman for a Beagle will adore him for being so sweet, gentle, fun, and playful. And she'll never take these qualities for granted. She'll appreciate his high degree of sociability and his desire to spend time with friends, family, and her. When his independent side comes out, she'll understand that and his need to pursue his interests. She'll keep a close eye on him or let him go and trust he'll come back, which of course he will when he has a wonderful loving home and companion to return to.

TYPICAL BEAGLE MAN: Jack's story, as told by himself:

High school graduation—my sweetheart and I were in love. We assumed the next step was getting married and starting a family. Within a year, we had a baby girl, Renee. Then we started to realize how little we had in common and how much we annoyed one another. Looking back on it, we were just young. We didn't know any better, and we picked each other mainly for superficial reasons. We tried to make it work, but things got worse and after three more years we called it quits.

Both of us later found other partners who were better suited for us. Our lives continued with new families, and Renee was included in both. During Renee's senior year, she started dating a boy named Chris. She had had a crush on him since middle school. One night, I overheard them talking about getting married. My stomach turned upside down, and I think my face turned green. Please, Renee, I thought, don't make the mistake your mother and I made. But what could I tell her? Why would she listen to me? I didn't listen to my parents. I called Renee's mother, Sheryl, and asked, "Sheryl, did you know Renee and her boyfriend are talking about getting married?"

Sheryl sighed heavily on the other end. "I was afraid of that. I asked Renee what she was planning to do after high school, and she said, "C'mon Mom, you know I'm going to college." But when I asked about her and Chris, she got evasive and clammed up.

"Jack, you're going to have to handle this. You talk to her. She'll listen to you."

Yeah, right, I thought. But I had no choice. I couldn't watch my daughter make the same mistake I had made. Still, I didn't want to squash her or her love for this boy. A few nights later I took her out for a quiet dinner, just the two of us. We did this occasionally, usually on birthdays or other special events. "Renee, I want to ask you to do something for me. It might be the hardest thing you ever have to do. And I hope you know I wouldn't ask if it weren't important to me."

"Wow, Dad," she said. "What's up?"

"I'm proud of you for starting college this fall, and I know you'll do well. I want you to have everything your heart desires, and I want you to be happy. I want you to have the experiences you need to have, and I want to help guide you along the way. Whether or not you accept my advice, just know that I will always love you." At this point I had to take a deep breath before continuing on.

"I know you and Chris love each other, and I heard you talking about getting married this summer. I think Chris is a nice person, but I'm concerned about you making the same mistake your mother and I made. I would like to ask you to wait. Go to college, and after you're finished if you still want to marry Chris, I will give you the best wedding I can."

Renee started crying and said all the things I had imagined she would say, "You don't understand, I love him. It's not like you and Mom. Can't you trust me?"

"Renee, all I'm doing is asking. Do what you need to do. But please think about it before getting married."

"Okay, Dad." And that was that. They continued to date, but no mention was made to me or anyone else about a wedding. Then, one night, it happened.

Renee came in crying. She and Chris had had a fight and they broke up. Apparently, this moment had been building for months but peaked when Chris got drunk at a party and started making fun of Renee in front of their friends. Drinking at high school parties seemed cool, but Renee was tired of it and Chris wasn't. Renee was ready to focus on her studies, but Chris wanted to see who could chug the fastest.

I'm grateful for the faith Renee showed me, that she would trust me enough to wait before getting married . . . because I asked her to. I don't know what will happen next, but I have confidence in her and in myself.

FAMOUS BEAGLE MAN: Michael J. Fox as Ben Stone in *Doc Hollywood*

On his way to Hollywood to begin a job as a plastic surgeon, Ben wrecks his car and a fence in the small town of Grady. He's not too happy being stuck there, performing community service and waiting for his car to be fixed. But, being a cheerful, fun-loving Beagle, he makes the best of it. He soon falls for a local woman, Lou, whose beauty and feisty ways attract him. Like a true Beagle, hot on the trail, he does everything he can to win her over. Covering at the local doctor's office, he soon makes friends with the small-town residents.

QUALITIES:

DETERMINED AND TIRELESS IN HIS PURSUITS

LAID-BACK, EASYGOING GUY

SOCIAL WHEN HE WANTS TO BE

WORKS GREAT ALONE AND WITH OTHERS

FOR EXPERIENCED WOMEN DUE TO: INDEPENDENCE AND STUBBORNNESS

Behavior with children:

Exercise required:

Activity level:

Ease of training:

Sociability with strangers:

Affection level:

Playfulness:

Protectiveness:

Watchdog ability:

PHYSICAL CHARACTERISTICS: Bloodhound men have one of the most extreme hang-dog looks you will ever see. They are large, rugged men who look as if they could walk for miles. Appearances are of little concern to the Bloodhound man. He'll wear the most comfortable clothes he can find. He may even wear them until they wear out.

ABILITIES & INTERESTS: The Bloodhound man is at his best when it comes to tracking. He can find a trail and stay on it better and longer than any other breed of man. Searching for missing persons, criminals, information and such is his forte. "Tireless" and "persistent" describe his dedication to work. He can be very independent and prefers to do his thing without someone telling him what to do or how to do it. When he's not tracking, he may prefer to take it easy and relax. Reading, watching television, sitting in a boat and fishing are things he enjoys when he has the time. Some people make the mistake of thinking that all Bloodhound men do is lie around, and that's not true. They can be active when they are attracted to something. Exercise is important to these men, and they need it every day. For them, however, this could mean walking for an hour or more. They don't necessarily need hard physical exercise or athletic sports activities. Bloodhound men can be perfectly content exercising by themselves.

TRAINING: Training a Bloodhound man can be challenging, but rewarding if you like a challenge. This man is very independent and stubborn. He needs immense amounts of praise and rewards. He is, however, easy to train at tracking because he is such a natural at it. If you can find a way to work with his tracking desire, you might have a chance at getting him to do something. Another trick is to let him think it was his idea in the first place. Scolding him will have little effect. He'll just ignore you or wonder what your problem is. If you are clear in your communication with a Bloodhound man and give him the freedom to occasionally put his foot down and say "No," you'll have an easier time getting him to cooperate.

SOCIAL SKILLS: Bloodhound men can be very friendly at first, although they may not spend a great deal of time getting to know someone. If interested, they will visit and learn more from a person, and if not, they'll move on. Some people feel at ease when they meet a Bloodhound man, and others are cautious about approaching him. Either way, they'll eventually realize he is a sweetheart of a guy without a mean bone in his body. He'll have friends, especially buddies he can spend time with. At work, he can be independent, and he can work well with others if given the freedom to do what he needs to do. Children feel safe with a Bloodhound man because he is so gentle with them. He may not be very playful, but he'll put up with a lot of rough-house treatment. In a relationship this man can be extremely affectionate and loving. He will also be independent and may take off if he's hot on the trail.

TYPE OF WOMAN: The woman for a Bloodhound will be independent. She'll appreciate his ability to be focused and track for hours on end. She's willing to let him off his leash and return when he's ready. Whether or not he does what she asks will not matter to her. She's quite capable of taking care of things herself. Family and children will be important to her.

TYPICAL BLOODHOUND MAN: Nick's story, as told by himself:

I found my calling early in life. As a child I was always the "cop" in "Cops and Robbers." In a small town being a cop is not the glamorous profession it appears on TV. But it fits me. I'm a laid-back kind of guy who likes keeping the peace. Most of the conflicts we have can be talked out at home or the local burger joint. But there was one case that wasn't so easy.

Forty years ago we didn't have all the sophisticated equipment we have now, so we had to take a different approach. I was new on the job and eager to prove myself. A call came in from Mrs. Jenkins saying she'd found her husband in the field, dead. He had accidentally shot himself. I went out with Sheriff Taylor. When we got there, we found Mrs. Jenkins red-eyed from crying. She led us to the body, and we asked her what happened.

"Clint said he was going squirrel hunting. He left. I heard a shot but didn't think anything of it until Bess, the coonhound, started howling and wouldn't stop. After a half hour or so, I got tired of her racket and went down to check on things. When I got there I found Clint . . . dead."

From what we could tell, the story fit. The bullet entry and the way he was lying, seemed consistent with an accident. At the same time, being new and wanting to impress the Chief, I kept my eyes and ears open for anything that might shed light on the incident. Well, there was plenty of gossip. In a small town, everyone knows everyone else's business. Or if they don't, they make it sound like they do. Most of the town thought what had happened was purely an accident. There were a few, however, who thought it suspicious. This group said the Jenkins couple fought. And Mrs. Jenkins in particular had a "nasty temperament." They thought she did it, and being a clever woman, staged the whole thing to appear as an accident. Perhaps they were right. Just because that sort of event had never happened in our small town before didn't mean it couldn't happen.

About six months later, I was talking to Miss Annie, a teacher, on some business unrelated to the case. After a while though we started talking about Mrs. Jenkins, and Miss Annie shared some interesting news that I couldn't shake. She said the Jenkins' niece, Sandy, a senior whom she taught, was struggling in school. Miss Annie was surprised to see this bright young girl fading and sinking.

I asked her, "What was Sandy's relationship with Mr. Jenkins like? Was she close to him and mourning his death?"

"No," Miss Annie said. "The families got together, and I thought Mrs. Jenkins and Sandy were close. But her relationship with Mr. Jenkins wasn't close enough to cause this type of spiral downhill."

I showed up at school a few days later and called Sandy out of class. The principal gave me permission to use her office. It didn't take much questioning for Sandy to start crying. And within half an hour, she had spilled the story. It seems Mrs. Jenkins had planned the whole murder and had coerced Sandy into being an accomplice. The guilt was destroying her. Fate, destiny, a sixth sense that a wrong had been committed, whatever you want to call it, I believe it led me to the truth.

I never had a case as big as that one again, fortunately. But many times since, I have relied on my intuition, determination, and patience to solve mysteries. Aside from my family, there is nothing that brings greater joy to my life than being a sheriff in a small town. You could call me the local Bloodhound.

FAMOUS BLOODHOUND MAN: Joe Friday on *Dragnet*

Friday, a detective with the L.A. police department, always gets his man. He works well with others, but he's independent and will go against others if need be. Relentless in his pursuit, he'll stay up all hours of the night, forsaking sleep when he's hot on a case. Methodical in his approach, he doesn't rush things. At the same time, he trusts his "hunches." Like when he knows someone is telling a lie . . . he can just tell. And he'll sniff the trail of a criminal until he tracks down his man.

THE BORZOI MAN

QUALITIES:

    ALOOF AND INDEPENDENT
    DETERMINED PURSUIT OF HIS INTERESTS
    LAID-BACK AND MELLOW
    SENSITIVE

FOR EXPERIENCED WOMEN DUE TO: INDEPENDENCE AND STUBBORNNESS

Behavior with children:

Exercise required:

Activity level:

Ease of training:

Sociability with strangers:

Affection level:

Playfulness:

Protectiveness:

Watchdog ability:

PHYSICAL CHARACTERISTICS: Borzoi men, also known as Russian Wolfhounds, are tall, lean, and look very aerodynamic. In their teens, they may slouch and seem uncomfortable in the tall bodies they acquired. As adults, they appear very aristocratic and carry themselves well. They may appear distant and aloof, which they can be, but when you get to know them, they can be very open and friendly. They are stronger than they appear to be.

ABILITIES & INTERESTS: Borzoi men are visually stimulated and love the chase. This may be women or art or stocks or any activity that they have a passion for. They can be completely absorbed and, once on a trail, they rarely can be called back. Although they will pursue their interests with passion, they truly enjoy spending quiet time either reading a book, watching television, or meditating. They can be great leaders because they are independent, intelligent, and people look up to them. Spiritual pursuits are important to most Borzoi men, and they have a strong connection to nature. Borzoi men need to run. They will adapt if confined but they can become irritable if cooped up for too long.

TRAINING: A Borzoi man can be extremely challenging to train because he is extremely independent. People sometimes mistakenly assume he is not intelligent because he can be inattentive. A Borzoi man is very intelligent, and this adds to the management challenge because he cleverly figures out ways not to obey. Training a Borzoi is like training a cat. It can be done, but it takes more praise, reward, and patience than most people are willing to spend. A Borzoi man can also be very sensitive. One word of criticism can undo weeks of praise. You must be prepared to give chase or let go of your Borzoi man if you let him off leash, because he will chase after anything of interest to him. If you are willing and know how to please a Borzoi man, you may find that you enjoy the challenge.

SOCIAL SKILLS: Borzoi men may appear aloof and distant, and some truly are. There are others who are very friendly and outgoing once they get to know someone and like the person. People often look up to these men and will put them on a pedestal. Borzoi men enjoy the role of leader, but they also need friends who understand their more down-to-earth, silly side. They like having close friends but, being so independent, they can spend a lot of time by themselves before realizing they miss the company of others. They can be wonderful with children. And when they tire of them, that's that: they'll move on, ignore them or, in rare instances, snap at them. In a relationship, they can be loyal and devoted to the person they love. At the same time, they may look at other women and perhaps give chase.

TYPE OF WOMAN: The woman best suited for a Borzoi man is very independent and likes to take care of things herself. She'll appreciate it when he helps out but will not require much from him. Jealousy is a trait she should be without. She must be capable of letting him run and do his thing while she does hers. He can be very cuddly and loving but usually when he is in the mood. If a woman appreciates the combination of a man, horse, dog, and cat, she'll love a Borzoi man.

TYPICAL BORZOI MAN: Lance's story, as told by his wife, Jeannette:

It was a late night in May and I was flying home on Southwest Airlines, but first I had a layover in Dallas, Texas. Sitting in the Love Field airport, I was thinking of my boyfriend with whom I had spent the weekend. We had decided to further our relationship, which meant quitting my job and leaving my house to go live with him. At that moment, in the airport, I looked up and noticed this tall, slender, attractive, mysterious-looking man and I felt deeply attracted to him. Shame on me! I thought and looked away.

Only a few people were on the flight and, since we could sit where we liked, I looked forward to using three seats to sleep. I sat by the window and closed my eyes. All of a sudden, I looked up wide-eyed just as the attractive man entered the plane. Dismissing him from my thoughts I closed my eyes again. Then I sensed someone sitting in the aisle seat—what a bother! I wanted to lie down. From my peripheral vision I realized it was the same man. Regardless, I wanted to sleep, not visit. Fortunately, he closed his eyes and went to sleep. Because he was asleep, I decided to lie down in the two seats, which meant my head was by his hip. I was just about to drift off to sleep when I imagined his hand caressing my cheek. Two seconds later that's what happened! He acted as if it was an accident, as if his hand slipped off the armrest onto my cheek. The rest of the flight was uneventful.

When we landed, this man turned to me and said, "Hi, I'm Lance Wright."

I was feeling curious as I shook his hand. "Jeannette Pingenot."

"Are you listed in the phone book?"

"Yes, but only for a month. I'm moving."

He gazed at me with piercing eyes. "A month isn't very long."

"No, it isn't." Suddenly I felt butterflies in my stomach and heard myself say, "But a lot can happen in a month."

Why did I say that?

As we walked off the plane, he kept staring at me with those piercing eyes, and I kept staring back. I felt as if he had me in a trance. What am I doing? I have a boyfriend. "Well, Lance, it was nice to meet you. I have to be at work, the Texas Water Commission, 7:00 tomorrow morning." Then without looking back, I left the airport and Lance.

The next morning at work, 7:15 AM, the phone rang.

Thinking of Lance from the night before, I answered dreamily. "Hello?"

"Hi, Jeannette, this is Lance from the airport, remember me? I was wondering if you'd like to have dinner with me tonight."

I about knocked over my morning tea. "This is fast."

"Well, you said we only have a month."

"Where would you take me?"

"How about Mother's?"

Again I felt butterflies in my stomach. Austin was a large city, and out of all the restaurants, Mother's was my favorite. At Mother's, Lance told me my birthday month, day, and year, saying he had dreamed it the night before. He reminded me of my dog, a Borzoi that had died two years earlier. Lance was calm, intelligent, attractive, cat-like, sensitive, independent, mysterious, and subtly affectionate.

What I experienced with Lance was magical, and I felt as if I had discovered a long-lost friend. I had found "Mr. Wright." Actually "Dr.," since he is a Network Spinal Analysis chiropractor. Within one week, I broke up with my boyfriend. Normally, I would not recommend what we did but within two weeks, we moved in together. It took a little longer for us to marry. After twelve years, I continue to be in awe of the ease with which we relate to and enjoy one another. I am grateful for his sensitive nature that intrigued me and his hound instinct that led him to me.

FAMOUS BORZOI MAN: Johnny Depp in *Chocolat*

Johnny Depp plays an aloof, cat-like gypsy. As a sighthound, he's quick to notice an attractive woman. He gives chase, although subtly, with a could-care-less attitude. He's completely indifferent to how others view him, so he's not out to please. He does what he wants, how he wants. Given his freedom, he returns in the end.

Qualities:

INDEPENDENT BUT SUPPORTIVE

LAID-BACK

WILLING TO COMMUNICATE IN A CALM MANNER

DIGGER (FOR INFO, ETC.)

FINE FOR NOVICE WOMEN

Behavior with children:

Exercise required:

Activity level:

Ease of training:

Sociability with strangers:

Affection level:

Playfulness:

Protectiveness:

Watchdog ability:

PHYSICAL CHARACTERISTICS: Dachshund men are long and lean. They have one of those "you can trust me" looks, and yet there is a twinkle in their eye that can make one wonder. Tough and self-confident, they tend to carry themselves with pride and dignity.

ABILITIES & INTERESTS: A Dachshund man will excel at digging and going after things, whether it be information or some tangible object. He is very curious and tenacious in his pursuits. Sometimes he can appear or even become obsessive-compulsive. Usually it is because he sees something others don't and he will not give up the pursuit. Dachshund men are also very playful and love to have fun. When he's in the mood, he will kick back, laugh, and enjoy himself. Exercise is not that important to him but is beneficial, especially if his activities are not physically demanding.

TRAINING: It may be difficult to train a Dachshund man since he can be somewhat independent and is sensitive. Be gentle but firm with him. Whining and yelling will get a woman nowhere. This man may require more tricks than just praise. Try using some of his favorite activities or appropriate gifts as rewards for excellent behavior. He will listen if you present the facts and ask for his cooperation. Whether or not he decides to do as you ask will oftentimes ultimately be up to him. He can be mischievous and will use his sense of humor to divert you from his inappropriate behavior. Be careful about letting him use this ploy too often. There are times when the best tactic is to just laugh and appreciate his comical side. It definitely beats getting into a tug-of-war match with him that cannot be won.

SOCIAL SKILLS:
Dachshund men tend to be wary of strangers, and going to social events where there will be new people may not appeal to them. Dachshund men can be independent but will gladly spend time with those they trust. They are very selective in the people they choose to associate with. Their circle of friends may not be large, but they will usually be strong connections. Although they can be childlike, they usually take time to warm up to children and do best with older children. In a relationship, Dachshund men can be affectionate and playful when they want to be.

TYPE OF WOMAN:
The best mate for a Dachshund man is a calm, independent, consistent woman who is intelligent and loving. She must accept his obsession, whatever it may be, and his need to pursue it. Because a Dachshund man is not especially social, a woman would either want to have the same preference for new people or at least accept him the way he is.

TYPICAL DACHSHUND MAN:
Juan's story, as told by his wife, Alejandra:

Early on in our relationship—"The Salad Days"—Juan and I were having a moderate disagreement. We had agreed to meet in a neutral place to discuss our options. Just then a long-gone, never-missed, ex-boyfriend appeared on the scene making all kinds of demands. I called Juan to explain that I was unfortunately detained by Roberto and could not make our appointment. Just as conversation with Roberto began to escalate into something experience told me would be exceptionally unpleasant, in strolled the calm, cool, and collected Juan. Unobtrusively, but with energy and style, he walked up beside me and without a word, slipped his arm around my waist. At that moment, everything was over. Roberto was gone, as was Juan and my rather silly argument. Juan never fights my battles for me, but he always catches me before I fall. He knows what I need or want before I do. Although it seems to me that his sacred duty as a man is to make me crazy, he is still my Prince, my Champion.

FAMOUS DACHSHUND MAN: David Duchovny as Agent Fox Mulder on *The X-Files*

Mulder's obsession is with finding the truth. He'll do whatever it takes to find it, including disobeying direct orders from his superiors in the FBI. He is independent and can work on his own but prefers the company of his colleague, Dana Scully, whom he's come to trust. Mulder has a great sense of humor, which comes out in the most unlikely instances. For example, in one episode, he and Scully pretend to be married suburbanites in an under-cover FBI assignment and he delights in holding hands and acting like the lovebug to play the role even though it irritates her.

QUALITIES:

INDEPENDENT AND HEADSTRONG

MULTITALENTED

CONFLICT BETWEEN PLEASING HIMSELF VERSUS ANOTHER

DESIRE TO CHASE AFTER HIS INTEREST

FOR EXPERIENCED WOMEN DUE TO: INDEPENDENCE AND STUBBORNNESS

Behavior with children:	🦴🦴
Exercise required:	🦴🦴
Activity level:	🦴🦴
Ease of training:	🦴
Sociability with strangers:	🦴🦴
Affection level:	🦴🦴
Playfulness:	🦴🦴
Protectiveness:	🦴🦴🦴
Watchdog ability:	🦴🦴🦴

PHYSICAL CHARACTERISTICS: Norwegian Elkhound men have a rugged outdoorsman look. They prefer to dress casual and wear what is most comfortable. Not that far removed from the wild, they can appear unkempt, but on them it looks good. Their eyes have an alert quality that is ever-watchful and takes everything in. At the same time, people might wonder what they are thinking, because they seem to be somewhere else.

ABILITIES & INTERESTS: These men excel in many areas. Norwegian Elkhound men love the hunt and tend to take on large prey, whether it's a project, cause, or person. They are tireless in their pursuit and are still going when others have quit. When they finally stop, however, they can really kick back and relax. Another ability Elkhound men have is pulling heavy loads for long distances across harsh terrain. Although they can handle a heavy load, they will stop if pushed too hard. The ever-attentive Elkhound man can be protective, but rarely overly protective. He tends to notice when something is amiss long before others do. He has a keen sense of what's going on around him at all times. Elkhound men enjoy being outdoors and letting their wild side come out. Outdoor exercise tends to be their favorite. Ball sports may or may not be of much interest.

TRAINING: Training an Elkhound man can be both easy and challenging. He wants very much to please and will try his best. At the same time, he can be very independent and stubborn. When he's hot on the trail, he can be completely unresponsive to any request. But when he's done, he'll do what's asked of him. It's difficult for him to understand that this upsets some women. He's just doing what he feels is necessary. He may not understand that his priorities are different from those of the woman he's with. Praise is very important to an Elkhound man. Criticism does not work well for this very sensitive guy.

SOCIAL SKILLS: Elkhound men tend to be friendly but not overly so. They may take some time warming up to a complete stranger. They are excellent judges of character. If they don't like someone, then pay attention and use caution. Once they've decided they like someone, they can be very friendly and open. They will usually have friends, but they are so independent they may not need to spend a lot of time with them. In times of stress, they will often turn to nature and the outdoors rather than to friends. Once they've bonded with someone, they can be extremely devoted. Children may or may not be of interest to these men. If they have children, they can be good fathers but may need their space more than some other daddies. In a relationship, these men can be very loving and devoted. They may not need much attention from a woman, but they will gladly take a lot if a woman has it to give.

TYPE OF WOMAN: The best woman for a Norwegian Elkhound man will be independent and enjoy an independent man. She'll appreciate his love of the outdoors and need to connect with nature. She will study his behavior with children, if that is important to her. When he goes on the hunt, she will have patience until he returns.

TYPICAL NORWEGIAN ELKHOUND MAN: Bryce's story, as told by Desmona:

As a musician and a bachelor, Bryce found the world easy and fun, especially when it came to women. When I, Desmona, arrived on the scene, he had no real desire to settle down and commit to a long-term relationship. We had a wonderful relationship and connected on a very deep level. Still, Bryce was not sure he wanted to make that leap of commitment. I finally gave Bryce the ultimatum—commit to me or I'm leaving. He couldn't take that step, so true to my word I left for Saudi Arabia to travel and work with the royal family. We made an agreement before I left that we would date around. And if we were going out with someone for a third date, then we would let the other person know.

I was gone for six months. When I returned, Bryce called. "Hey, Desmona, I left my wrench at the house. I was wondering . . . could I swing by and pick it up?" "Sure, come get it. I'll leave it on the front porch."

A couple of days later he called back, "Hey, Desmona, me again. I hate to trouble you again, but I need my hedge clippers."

"No problem, Bryce, they'll be on the front porch."

This "calling for his tools" went on for a while until he finally called and said, "Desmona, I'm really missing you and . . . I would love to come see you."

Feeling deeply touched, I invited him over. It was like a scene right out of Romeo and Juliet. When he drove up, I was on the balcony surrounded by lush plants. The moment he saw me he said, "Desmona, all this time we've been apart, I've missed you. I asked for a sign, and seeing you on the balcony when I drove up made my stomach turn upside down. I feel like you're truly the one."

My heart just melted.

After he came up and we talked, we agreed to go out on a date. At the same time he informed me that he had gone out with another woman, and their next date would be their third. Since that date was already scheduled, he went out with her first, but told her that night he was in love with someone else and could not see her anymore.

We started dating again. Bryce was more committed this time but still not poised to marry me. For the second time in our relationship, I told him, "Bryce, I need more than this. I love you, but I'm not willing to date you unless I know marriage is in our future. You have to make a decision." A few days later, we went to church and the minister said, "Until a person is willing to commit fully to something, whatever that may be, he will never fully succeed at it." Talk about a sign. We walked out of the church, and Bryce walked right into the middle of a busy street with cars buzzing by him right and left. He looked at me with tears in his eyes and said, "All right, Desmona, I'll do it. I'll marry you."

I thank God for the choice Bryce made. My life has been more beautiful with Bryce as my husband.

FAMOUS NORWEGIAN ELKHOUND MAN: Russell Crowe as Terry Thorn in *Proof of Life*

Terry plays a kidnapping and ransom negotiator who meets up with an attractive woman, Alice, whose husband is kidnapped in Tecala. Like a true Elkhound, he's willing to take on an opponent that is bigger than himself and maintain pursuit until his task is completed. Independent, headstrong, and confident, he lets nothing stand in his way. Despite the growing attraction between him and Alice, he maintains respect for her and her husband's life.

QUALITIES:

USES MANY SENSES WHEN ON THE HUNT

VERY PROTECTIVE FOR A HOUND MAN

FEARLESS AND TOUGH

MAKES HIS OWN RULES

FOR EXPERIENCED WOMEN DUE TO: INDEPENDENCE, STUBBORNNESS, AND AGGRESSIVENESS

Behavior with children:	🦴🦴
Exercise required:	🦴🦴🦴
Activity level:	🦴
Ease of training:	🦴
Sociability with strangers:	🦴
Affection level:	🦴🦴
Playfulness:	🦴🦴
Protectiveness:	🦴🦴🦴
Watchdog ability:	🦴🦴🦴

PHYSICAL CHARACTERISTICS: Ridgeback men have deep, penetrating eyes that can see inside one's soul, or so it seems. These are lean, muscular, athletic men who carry themselves with poise and grace. Their friendly appearance can belay their protective qualities. Most of the time, these men prefer nice, casual sporting attire.

ABILITIES & INTERESTS: Rhodesian Ridgeback men are natural hunters. Fearless, they will take on the "lions" that other co-workers will avoid. Unique among the hound men, they use many of their senses when they're on the chase. They'll use their visual senses when they can. Failing that, they'll use their sense of smell, and when needed, a sixth sense that eludes others. They are talented problem solvers and know how to get things done. Just don't expect them to follow orders unless it suits them. They play chess or video games for intellectual stimulation. Another characteristic that sets them apart from the typical hound man is their strong protective instinct. Their hunting abilities, combined with their protective nature, make for a powerful, sometimes fierce man. Athletic activities are a must for these men. It doesn't always matter what form of exercise they get, just so long as they get it . . . often.

TRAINING: A Rhodesian Ridgeback man requires a special woman and a special approach. To start with, he is extremely intelligent. Although this may seem like a blessing, it has its challenges, mainly because he is independent, headstrong, determined, and focused. Regardless of how you approach him, he may or may not respond immediately. Be firm and consistent. Use his playful nature to get work done. Like making a game out of painting the bedroom—whose wall looks the best and gets done the fastest. A hint: Letting him win will make him more likely to play in the future. Don't ever become abusive with a Ridgeback man. At the same time, don't put up with aggression from him. If need be, get professional help.

SOCIAL SKILLS: Rhodesian Ridgebacks are independent and can work well with others if they have a mission that requires a concerted effort. Otherwise they prefer to work alone. Generally they are cautious around strangers. Don't expect them to enjoy parties and events where they are expected to be social with strangers. They will have one or possibly a few close friends. With these friends, they are devoted and loyal. Ridgeback men can make loving, affectionate, playful fathers. Watch for overly protective behavior and rambunctious behavior that can get too rough for younger or more sensitive children. Extremely loyal and devoted, these men will "stand by their women." They will be affectionate and playful with those they love and trust.

TYPE OF WOMAN: The woman for a Ridgeback man will be strong, self-confident, and able to take care of herself. She'll appreciate his devotion, affection, and playfulness but will not expect much obedience. Knowing he may become overly protective, she'll encourage this behavior only when appropriate. Otherwise, she'll encourage him to be more relaxed and trusting. She'll appreciate his need to "hunt."

TYPICAL RHODESIAN RIDGEBACK MAN: Captain Trip's story, as told by Jeff:

I grew up in Missouri, but I became a man in Iraq. It was during the first Desert Storm. Like a number of my close friends, I signed up to become a Marine. We didn't expect to see any real action. We did it to help pay for college. Life has its own sense of humor, and right after signing up, SURPRISE! We were going to Iraq to engage in a conflict we knew little about.

Captain Trip was also from Missouri, but he wasn't like us. He wasn't in it for the short haul; he was made for the military. The desert seemed to suit him as well. When the rest of us were wilting, he was running as if it were early springtime back home in Jefferson City. He pushed the edge, and regardless of the adversity, he never showed any signs of fear. Even though he wasn't much older than us, we completely trusted him with our lives—he was that kind of man. We knew he would get us through any conflict or die trying.

On a sweltering day during a routine patrol, we spotted dust in the distance. Captain Trip decided to have us check it out. As we approached, we realized it had been a trap and there behind us were Iraqi soldiers in two jeeps. "Jeff, we're sitting ducks out here in the open. Get us to those buildings on our left. Be prepared, men! We don't know what's there, but we sure know what's in front and behind us." Fortunately for us, the buildings were empty. We radioed for help but got only static. Since we had wandered a distance from our routine patrol, we were concerned about help finding us any time soon.

The Iraqi soldiers kept us holed up there throughout the day. We had enough water, because Captain Trip always made us bring extra. As night approached, one of the men started to lose it. With the exception of Captain Trip, we were all scared. "Boys, we take care of our own. Troops will be out here soon to bring us back in. I understand you're afraid, that's nothing to be ashamed of. The question is, what do you do with that fear? Do you let it fester inside and weaken you, or do you turn it around and let the adrenaline from it make you stronger? It's the choices we make now and throughout our lives that determine the men we will be in the future. Who do you want to be in the future? Be that now." It may not have been the best, most rousing speech ever spoken, but in that moment, it was what we needed to hear. We pulled together, staying strong. And, true to his word, reinforcements showed up around six that morning.

When our country went back into Iraq for the second time, I was married and had three children. I heard through a friend that Captain Trip was now a Colonel. Lucky were the men under his command, I thought. It wasn't much later that I heard how he had single-handedly taken on ten Iraqi soldiers and managed to get some valuable information that made a difference in the war. I'm glad I didn't have to go back to war, but if I had, I'd have wanted to go under the command of Colonel Trip, the man who taught me the meaning of the word "man."

FAMOUS RHODESIAN RIDGEBACK MAN: John Cusack as Martin Blank in *Grosse Pointe Blank*

Martin returns to his hometown after skipping out on his ex-girlfriend on prom night years before. Hired as a hit man to take out her father, he's torn between his mission to hunt her father down and his love and protective feelings for her. He can be ruthless and cunning. At the same time, he can be devoted and loyal. Despite being jilted by him on prom night, his ex-girlfriend still can't escape his deep eyes, mysterious persona, and intellectually stimulating conversation.

8

THE WORKING GROUP

MEN IN THE WORKING GROUP are able to work hard with intense focus when needed. They also have the tendency to be protective of what is theirs. They respect strong authority figures and will gladly work to please them.

AKITA: These guys can be sweet and can also be extremely, sometimes overly, protective. They take their business very seriously.

BOXER: Looks can be deceiving. Although they appear tough, these guys are usually bouncy, playful friends who just want to be loved.

DOBERMAN PINSCHER: These guys are serious protectors. Few people are brave enough to approach a Doberman without first asking if he bites. Treat them with love and respect, and they will return the fond regard.

GREAT DANE: Although these are big guys and can appear intimidating, most are gentle and laid back. They can be very playful.

MASTIFF: These large guys don't have to do much as guards. They can stand there, and that's enough. Of course, they prefer to lie down, and, while so disposed, they appreciate a nice pat or two.

ROTTWEILER: These are tough guys you don't want to mess with. They can also be great big cuddly teddy bears, if they like you.

SAINT BERNARD: It may not look as if this breed would do much because they love to lie around. But in an emergency they're courageous, tough, and hardworking.

SCHNAUZER: These hardworking guys are watchful of others but playful with those they love. They are very task-oriented.

SIBERIAN HUSKY: These guys are not that far removed from wolves, so expect a little wildness. They can pull very heavy loads and sometimes take on too much.

QUALITIES:

PROTECTIVE

REGAL LOOKS AND ATTITUDE

DISTRUSTFUL OF MOST STRANGERS

AGILE AND QUICK WHEN NEEDED

FOR EXPERIENCED WOMEN DUE TO: INDEPENDENCE, STUBBORNNESS, AND AGGRESSIVENESS

	Rating (bones)
Behavior with children:	1
Exercise required:	2
Activity level:	1
Ease of training:	2
Sociability with strangers:	1
Affection level:	2
Playfulness:	2
Protectiveness:	3
Watchdog ability:	3

PHYSICAL CHARACTERISTICS: The Akita man is a powerful, tough-looking man who can also appear quite regal. He doesn't necessarily look fierce as compared to some guard breeds of men. However, he is intimidating enough that people are cautious about approaching him. There is a slightly wild look about him, hinting at an independent spirit. He tends to be a neatly-dressed man who spends time on his appearance.

ABILITIES & INTERESTS: Akita men are powerful, tough protectors. They can sense danger and will do whatever is necessary to protect themselves, those they love, their ideas, and their things. Few people are willing to take on an Akita. They make formidable adversaries. It may not take much for these men to jump into a fight. They work well in the police force and will follow orders when they respect the person giving them. At the same time, they have been known to twist the rules to fit their needs. When they are not being protective, these men can be very laid back and enjoy taking it easy, and, when in the mood, they can be playful. They are intelligent and enjoy activities that employ their minds. Because they are independent, they will often find things that they can do alone. Exercise is beneficial for these strong men, and they usually prefer lifting weights or some activity that keeps them strong and fit.

TRAINING: An Akita man can certainly be trained, but you must know what you are doing and know how to approach him. Combine powerful, independent, and stubborn and you understand why you must use caution. If you are independent, self-confident, clear in your communication, and respectful of an Akita man, you can have a very easy time working with him. Most challenging would be an insecure woman or a woman who comes on too strong. When pushed too hard, an Akita man can be dangerous. Praise and rewards work well with him, with the understanding that he may be slow to respond. You should ignore unwanted behavior and, if he ever acts overly aggressive, you should be prepared to get outside help.

SOCIAL SKILLS: Meeting strangers is not an Akita's strong suit. He tends to be suspicious of people. It may be hard to get to know an Akita unless he wants you to. Sometimes an Akita man will be more open. It depends on his past experiences, and especially on his childhood. He may have a friend or two, and with them his loyalty will run deep; otherwise, he has little need for friends. At work, he may be known as the loner or maverick because he does so well on his own. With children, he can be too powerful. If he wants to have children, watch him closely with other people's children. This will give you some idea what to expect. Keep in mind that he may not be that good with other people's children but be excellent with his own. He may also be a strict and hard disciplinarian, so be prepared. In a relationship, he is extremely devoted and can be affectionate with someone he really bonds to. He may be protective, so you need to know if this is a trait you can appreciate or not.

TYPE OF WOMAN: The best woman for an Akita man will want a man to protect and watch over her. She'll enjoy having a strong man around even if he doesn't respond the minute she makes a request. She will be independent and self-confident. Before having children, she will watch him carefully with children and make sure he wants children. She will respect his aloofness with strangers and not force him into uncomfortable situations.

TYPICAL AKITA MAN: Jay's story, as told by himself:

I became a karate black belt at age 15. Winning tournaments was my passion. Later, I studied other forms of martial arts: Aikido, Tae Kwon Do, and Qi Kung. With all this knowledge and ability, I've only once come close to using it.

I put aside some of my martial arts competitions when I became the Safety Inspector for a large chemical plant. Shortly after that, I married and had two beautiful daughters. My eldest daughter, Rachel, was precious to me because she was the first, and maybe because I didn't think I would like being a father. Other people's children could annoy me, but Rachel never did. I would do anything for her, and oftentimes I was accused of being overly protective.

Her first year at college was rough for me. I missed her and worried about her. One of my worst fears was confirmed in the spring. Rachel called, distraught, "Daddy, please come get me."

"What's going on, Sugar? Are you hurt? Sick? What?"

"Please, Daddy, just come. I don't want to talk about it on the phone."

Her school was four hours away and it was 1:00 AM, but I jumped into the car and took off, driving faster than my Taurus had ever been driven.

When I arrived, she collapsed into my arms and cried for what felt like hours. I just let her cry, knowing that below the deep end of her pool of tears lay a tough story to tell.

"Daddy, I went out with this guy I met at a party. He seemed nice and all. He took me to eat at a nice restaurant and we were having a great time. Then he took me to his apartment and I said he should take me home. But he said he needed to pick something up and it would only take a moment. So I went in with him, and then he . . ."

More sobbing, but I just held her and said, "It's okay, Rachel, take your time, I'm here." What she told me made me furious. I wanted to kill this kid named Jeff, and I knew it would be easy for me to do so with my bare hands. "Rachel, I want you to tell me where this boy lives. I'm going to go pay him a visit."

I got Jeff's address and took off. I didn't know what I would do when I got there, I just went.

At Jeff's apartment, I knocked on the door. No answer, so I knocked again. Finally a groggy boy answered the door. "Yeah?"

"Are you Jeff?" I asked.

"Yeah, do you have any idea what time . . . ."

I slammed him against the wall and held him in a grip that felt good. Blood rushing through my fingertips urged me to squeeze harder but I resisted. "Jeff, I'm Rachel's dad, and I heard about what happened tonight. I'll give you the chance to call the cops right now and turn yourself in. If not, you'll wish you had. In fact you'll wish, when I'm finished with you, that I had just killed you."

"All right, all right," he sobbed. "I'll call them."

After Jeff was booked, and I calmed down and talked to Rachel some more, I realized if this kid went to prison, chances are he'd only serve a little time, be back out, and maybe do it again. So I talked to Rachel, met with his lawyer and parents, and we all agreed that if he would get help at an institute that has a proven track record for rehabilitating young men, and if he would perform a year of service, then Rachel wouldn't press charges.

A year after the incident, Rachel showed me a letter Jeff sent her.

Dear Rachel,

A year has gone by, and I've never stopped regretting what I did to you. I read a story the other day. I'd like to share it with you. A man, John, did an injustice to another man, Peter. John said, "Peter, I'm sorry for what I've done. How can I make it up to you?" Peter replied, "Go find a feather pillow. Cut it open and scatter the feathers to the wind." John did as Peter asked and returned, saying, "I did as you asked, Peter." To which Peter replied, "Now go find all those feathers and bring them to me." "I can't do that," John said. "That's impossible." "Right," said Peter. "Just like you can never undo what you have done to me."

When I read that I thought of you, Rachel. I can never undo what I've done to you. All I can offer is that, because of you and your dad and your kind hearts, that what I did to you—I will never do that to another woman.

I give you my regrets for the person I was and my thanks for the person I am.

Sincerely,

Jeff

FAMOUS AKITA MAN: McCloud in *Highlander*

McCloud is a born fighter. His motto is "There can be only one." Meaning he and others of his type (immortals) will fight each other to the death until only one survives. For this reason, he is distrustful of strangers. He is very protective and loving toward those he trusts. McCloud can also be very gentle and easygoing when he does not feel threatened.

QUALITIES:

PLAYFUL—PHYSICALLY AND MENTALLY

PROTECTIVE BUT NOT AGGRESSIVE

TENACIOUS

ABLE TO TUNE THE WORLD OUT

FINE FOR NOVICE WOMEN

Behavior with children:

Exercise required:

Activity level:

Ease of training:

Sociability with strangers:

Affection level:

Playfulness:

Protectiveness:

Watchdog ability:

PHYSICAL CHARACTERISTICS: Boxer men may appear intimidating to others because they can have a serious look on their faces. They spend a lot of time deep in thought, and the lines around their faces reflect this level of concentration. They usually stay in decent shape because of their active lifestyles. They prefer casual, comfortable attire.

ABILITIES & INTERESTS: Boxer men can be excellent protectors because they are very alert and aware of what is going on around them. At the same time, they are not overly aggressive and will engage in a fight only when protecting loved ones or cherished objects. These men are intelligent and possess many talents. The important thing is finding activities that keep them engaged, because they are easily bored. They have tenacity, like the intensity of many terriers, and once they grab hold of an idea or project, they may not let go. In a game of tug-of-war, they will almost always win. Boxer men love to play and will completely throw themselves into a playful wrestling match, a board game, or some outdoor sport. The challenge can be to make them stop, but when they finally do quit, they love to kick back and relax. They can easily go from one extreme of play to rest.

TRAINING: Training a Boxer man can be challenging for a number of reasons. One is that he can be so caught up in his own agenda, he loses sight of anyone else's. Another is his slightly independent ways and occasional stubborn streak. Also challenging is his deep desire for play. It can be tough to make him focus when he's in the play mode. The last obstacle in training this man is his sensitive nature, of which most people are unaware at first, because Boxers are such tough men. But when it comes to communication, one harsh word can take days to heal. Praise works wonders with him, and although it may not work absolute miracles in training him, it will certainly prevent belligerent attitudes that can interfere with a harmonious life. Clear and consistent communication is important in working with a Boxer man. If you are prepared to do what needs to be done, not expect anything from a Boxer, and then are grateful when he does respond, you will find life much easier. Ultimately you will also find him more responsive.

SOCIAL SKILLS: Boxer men can be friendly, but they usually take their time warming up to someone. People may also be hesitant to come up to them at first. Most people aren't sure if these men are going to be friendly or not. After a Boxer warms up to a person and they become friends, the person will often wonder why he was ever intimidated by him. The Boxer man tends to be a good judge of character and will be wary of people who send out the wrong vibrations. Boxer men are excellent with children. They are so playful that they immediately get down to the level of whatever child they are playing with. Extremely patient and gentle, they make wonderful fathers. In a relationship, these men are very devoted and loyal. Again, they love to play and some women may be offended if the playfulness makes them feel that they are not being taken seriously. These men will do their best to be wonderful companions.

TYPE OF WOMAN: The woman most suited for a Boxer will appreciate his boisterous, playful nature. She will enjoy playing with him and will avoid overly competitive games such as tug-of-war, where she will lose. She will be very complimentary of him and will understand how difficult it is to train him. Independent and capable, she will not need him to take care of her, and yet she will understand his desire to protect her.

TYPICAL BOXER MAN: Lloyd's story, as told by his daughter, Mary:
    Every night, Dad would tuck us in, saying, "I love you. Sweet dreams.

I'll see you in the morning." He was always there for us—quiet and gentle, but very strong. Dad attended every one of our functions—talent shows, soccer games, piano recitals, and the like. Evenings, he would play games with us or put his arm around us while we watched TV. He adored us and Mom. Maybe he didn't always do what Mom wanted when and how she wanted it, but there was still no denying his love and devotion to her. One incident stands out in my mind where he proved it most.

Christmas at Granddad's was a family tradition. Every year our family, Dad's parents, and his four brothers along with their families would come together. Granddad ruled the family. What he said was law. Nobody ever went against him . . . ever. One year, we wanted to visit Mom's family for Christmas, and we had to have special permission from Granddad. He said yes, but only that one time, never again. On the particular Christmas family holiday I remember, Granddad called all the family into the living room. He did this occasionally, lecturing the family on some subject.

He began with, "Women are the root of all evil."

Oh boy, we thought, here we go.

"They are not to be trusted," Granddad went on. "Like in the Bible, it was Eve who was to blame. Women are all sluts. They use men to get what they want. If they find a better deal with someone else, they'll leave their husband. It's important to control your wives. Keep them in their place." All of a sudden, Dad, usually the quietest of the brothers, stood up to Granddad. "How dare you. You have no right to speak of my wife like that. She is a wonderful woman. I trust her, I love her, and I won't listen to another word! If you say one more rude, hurtful comment about women, me and my family are leaving. Your choice!" Stunned silence fell.

I don't remember who recovered and closed his mouth first. I only remember Granddad storming out of the room. He didn't talk to any of us the rest of that day, but nobody cared. Out of the five brothers, Dad was the only one who stood up to his dad that night. Later, my mom said, "Of all the things people have ever done for me or said to me, I have never felt so loved as I did when Lloyd stood up to his dad that day."

FAMOUS BOXER MAN: Jackie Chan as Detective Lee in *Rush Hour*

Detective Lee risks his life to save a young girl. She is special to him because he's protected her and trained her to protect herself. He has a tendency to do things his way regardless of orders. He doesn't unnecessarily start a fight, but if someone pushes, such as in the pool bar, he'll take care of himself. When he first meets Detective Carter, Detective Lee is not sure about him and takes his time sizing him up. It doesn't take long for him to recognize that Carter's desire and his are the same.

QUALITIES:

TOUGH AND STOIC

SENSITIVE BUT RESERVED

ATHLETIC

UNPREDICTABLE

FOR EXPERIENCED WOMEN DUE TO: AGGRESSIVENESS

Behavior with children:	🦴
Exercise required:	🦴 🦴
Activity level:	🦴 🦴 or 🦴 🦴 🦴
Ease of training:	🦴 🦴 or 🦴 🦴 🦴
Sociability with strangers:	🦴
Affection level:	🦴 🦴
Playfulness:	🦴 🦴
Protectiveness:	🦴 🦴 🦴
Watchdog ability:	🦴 🦴 🦴

PHYSICAL CHARACTERISTICS: Doberman Pinscher men usually have lean, muscular physiques. They have an intense, watchful look in their eyes and may appear distant and aloof. Many Dobermans are drawn to careers where they are required to wear a uniform. Even if they don't wear a uniform, they are usually neatly dressed.

ABILITIES & INTERESTS: Doberman men excel in the military, police force, or any career that places emphasis on following orders and being disciplined. They are well equipped for these fields because they have intelligence, endurance, strength, and courage. Ever watchful, they are extremely sensitive to suspicious people and situations. They enjoy playing the role of guardian and will eagerly watch over people, places, and objects that need protecting. If they do not choose a path in a guardian role, they need to work for a company or person they respect. If not, they will be challenging and will try to gain control. They require and enjoy physical activity, especially sports that they can do by themselves, such as jogging or lifting weights. They can be extremely competitive.

TRAINING: A Doberman man can be easily trained once you gain his trust. If he doesn't feel trusted and respected, he will forever challenge you. A woman strong in herself, who respects herself, will have his respect. If she tries to be controlling or covers up her own insecurities, he may see through her and, in turn, be a challenge. You must be aware of his extra-sensitive nature and be strong but gentle. In a relationship, the best approach is lots of love and praise. Harsh treatment can backfire, and a sweet Doberman man can turn combative when pushed. In the military or a similar setting he can take harshness and abuse, but a personal relationship is very different.

SOCIAL SKILLS: Doberman men can be unpredictable, so beware of and pay attention to their behavior. Doberman men can vary in their social temperaments. Some make excellent family men. Some do not. Some are trusting of others and some are not. Much depends on their background. With a Doberman man, it is especially important to spend time watching his actions before rushing into a serious relationship. Actions speak louder than words. Be prepared for a Doberman man to be protective. Some women would say they can be overly protective. Depending on a woman's needs, this protective nature could be a real plus. Usually, a stable Doberman will be watchful but rarely engage in fighting unless absolutely necessary. In a healthy relationship, he can be devoted and affectionate.

TYPE OF WOMAN: The woman best suited for a Doberman Pinscher man is a woman who appreciates a protective kind of guy—a guy dedicated to his work and a guy who may appear cool, rather distant and quiet, but who can be a sweetheart given enough love and respect. She will be confident and strong enough in herself that he can respect her.

TYPICAL DOBERMAN PINSCHER MAN: Joe's story, as told by his ex-girlfriend:
His dog was named Spike. His fish was named Spike. That about sums Joe up—tough guy. Especially on the outside. Extremely competent, he could accomplish anything he put his mind to. However, I didn't have a clue how to be in a relationship with him. If I'd known he was a Doberman man, it would have made our relationship less chaotic. But then I ask myself, if I'd known he was a Doberman man, would I have gotten involved in the first place? Not that I question how awesome Doberman men are— I question my ability to be in a relationship with a Doberman man.

One story can sum up a multitude of experiences. Like a true Doberman, Joe was protective—protective of me and his things. But even more, he was protective of his self–image. He said he had no fears. He projected confidence at all times and would never admit to ignorance on any subject. He could talk about his childhood and reveal deep emotions, even let a tear fall. But even at his most open, he wouldn't let go of his strong image of himself. Much of our conflict came from this tough, stoic behavior. I thought he was covering up insecurities.

But one day, after a particularly grueling bicycle race, as we drove home, he revealed a side of himself I had never seen. He said, "I'll never be as good a cyclist as Lance Armstrong, and I may never be as good as the other guys I ride with, but I'll continue to ride as hard as I can and be the best I can be." In that moment, I realized that whether his self-image was real or not, I had to admire his spirit and determination to be the best he could be.

Famous Doberman Pinscher Man: Tom Cruise as Pete "Maverick" Mitchell in *Top Gun*

In *Top Gun,* Tom Cruise plays a pilot for the U.S. Navy. In true Doberman form, he is cool, reserved, controlled, and quick to learn. He follows orders well, even though he shows a little rebelliousness now and then. It takes time for him to warm up to strangers, but he's very loyal and devoted to those he loves.

QUALITIES:

PROTECTIVE BUT NOT AGGRESSIVE

HE KNOWS HOW TO RELAX

GOOD PROBLEM SOLVER

GENTLE GIANT

FINE FOR NOVICE WOMEN

Behavior with children:

Exercise required:

Activity level:

Ease of training:

Sociability with strangers:

Affection level:

Playfulness:

Protectiveness:

Watchdog ability:

PHYSICAL CHARACTERISTICS: Great Dane men can appear large and intimidating at first glance. Their smiles and cheerful demeanor will put people at ease given a little time. Most Dane men are comfortable in casual dress although some prefer the black suit and tie look. When they are dressed up, they appear regal and tend to stand out in a crowd.

ABILITIES & INTERESTS: Great Dane men make excellent protectors, and yet they are not aggressive. It's mainly their look that keeps others at bay. If pushed, they are certainly capable of defensive action, but they have to be pushed hard. These men are very attentive and notice more than you might realize. They are intelligent and good at problem solving. If need be, when all else fails, they can use their strength to get their way. Most Great Dane men will choose the path of least resistance; they prefer a life of ease. Some people may accuse them of being couch potatoes or complain that they don't do enough. It's true that Great Dane men enjoy their leisure time, but they can have successful careers when their hearts are in it. Dane men enjoy exercise, and they like playing—sometimes a bit rough, though.

TRAINING: A Great Dane man is fairly easy to train because he is intelligent and wants to please. It takes a small amount of praise and reward to appeal to him. He can take a fair amount of criticism and harsh treatment, but be careful about pushing him in too tight a corner. He can lash out, although very rarely. Besides, he is so sweet and responds so much better to praise. The one challenge with training a Dane man is the speed at which he responds. He may take his time: "Why do today what you can put off till tomorrow?" can be his motto. However, he will eventually do what is asked of him.

SOCIAL SKILLS: Great Dane men tend to like people, but they may take their time warming up to someone at first. They are usually good judges of character and keep an eye on those they find suspicious. With friends, they are devoted and very playful. In a work environment, they tend to get along with everyone. These men are great with children. They may scare some children with their imposing size at first, but children soon get over that and have a great time playing with the Dane men. Be careful these men don't get too rough with small children. Great Danes sometimes don't realize how powerful they are. In a relationship, they are very loyal, loving, and playful. They will bend over backward to make a woman happy.

TYPE OF WOMAN: The woman for a Great Dane man will appreciate feeling safe with this gentle but powerful man. She'll praise him for his intelligence and willingness to please. His desire to take life slower and easier than some will not bother her. An early response or a later one will be acceptable to her.

TYPICAL GREAT DANE MAN: Warren's story, as told by his wife, Liz:

When Jeannette asked me to write a story about my husband of 30 years, I could not think of one great story. What must that say about my marriage? I mean, he has to have done something, right? But try as I might I couldn't think of anything. All I could think about were the things he hasn't done. Mainly, I wish he would find a better-paying job.

Despondent, I went to bed and asked my dreams to reveal some sweet, touching, emotional story about Warren. Well, I got my answer, but not what I expected. In the dream, I was sitting in a comfortable chair, and there was a screen on the wall—it was so big. Everything was life-size. All these scenes started flashing on the screen of Warren performing different activities for me.

One moment he was getting out of the car, and he put the seat back to where I keep it for myself. In the next scene, he was sweeping the floor while I was gone. Then, he went out of his way to buy a certain type of bread I wanted, because the store we usually shop at was out of it. I saw him cancel a golf game he had looked forward to all week, so he could instead stay home and help me with my mother who was ill and staying with us that week. These scenes just kept coming, one after another. By the end of the dream, I was exhausted.

When I woke up, I realized that for 30 years, I'd been so busy noticing all the things he doesn't do that I missed all the things he has done. He's so good-natured and he just keeps doing them regardless of how I treat him. What would happen if I started recognizing the things he does? And what would he do if I started showing him appreciation instead of complaining all the time? It's a scary thought, to change my behavior after 30 years. But it's even scarier not to.

FAMOUS GREAT DANE MAN: Shaggy in *Scooby Doo*

Shaggy and Scooby Doo are great buddies because they are so much alike. They are capable of warning Daphne, Thelma, and Fred of trouble. Shaggy and Scooby help the group in other ways, but given a choice, they prefer to hang out and eat. They are the extreme when it comes to being laid back. Go-getter is not a word to describe them. They redeem themselves by being fun, loving, sweetheart guys who are loyal and trustworthy. Thelma, Daphne, and Fred can count on Shaggy to come to their aid when necessary.

QUALITIES:

WARRIOR/PROTECTOR WHEN NEED BE

BIG, CUDDLY TEDDY BEAR

TOUGH BUT SENSITIVE

APPRECIATES MOVING IN THE SLOW LANE OF LIFE

FOR EXPERIENCED WOMEN DUE TO: STUBBORNNESS

Behavior with children: 🦴 🦴 🦴

Exercise required: 🦴 🦴

Activity level: 🦴

Ease of training: 🦴 🦴

Sociability with strangers: 🦴 🦴

Affection level: 🦴 🦴 🦴

Playfulness: 🦴

Protectiveness: 🦴 🦴 🦴

Watchdog ability: 🦴 🦴 🦴

PHYSICAL CHARACTERISTICS: Mastiff men are large, powerfully built men, and they look like the ultimate warrior. They prefer casual dress but will wear whatever attire is most appropriate for the battle they face. They can appear intimidating due to their size and look of self-confidence. They may not say much, but when they do, people listen.

ABILITIES & INTERESTS: Mastiff men are most inclined to lie around and take it easy. They like keeping an eye on things without having to do a lot of extra work. They are well equipped to guard and protect, in part because they are generally big, strong men, and they are courageous. They don't look for a fight. It has to come to them, but if it ever does, a Mastiff man is a solid wall of protection. Mastiff men make good football players and bouncers and are a good match in any other occupation where size and strength count. They are intelligent, so there are many other fields that may suit them as well. Whatever they do in life, they take their time in doing it and can appear to be moving slower than everyone around them. In a time of emergency or necessity, though, they can keep up with and even surpass others. Although they may not care to exercise, they need it.

TRAINING: A Mastiff man is a gentle sweetheart, but he will not win many obedience awards. He is intelligent but has a mind of his own. He can be stubborn, and the more you pull the more he will resist. A Mastiff man requires a strong, self-assured woman. In the wrong hands he can be aggressive and domineering. The best way to treat a Mastiff man is with lots of praise and love. Never become abusive, or you're asking for trouble.

SOCIAL SKILLS:

Mastiff men are adept at reading people, and they will take their time to assess a person before jumping into a conversation. If they trust the person and feel comfortable, they can be quite friendly. Mastiff men are not the most gregarious men. If you love the social scene, with lots of parties, you might think twice about choosing a Mastiff. He'll go if duty calls, but he would usually prefer to spend an evening with family and close friends. Even though they are not demanding of attention, Mastiff men like companionship. They will form close friendships that may last for years. If you give him time with friends, he'll appreciate it. He's a great family man. Children are safe with a Mastiff man, even though his size might at first intimidate a few. They'll soon lose their shyness when they look into his eyes. In a relationship, he can be extremely affectionate, loving, and loyal. At times, he can also be protective.

TYPE OF WOMAN:

The woman for a Mastiff man needs to be self-confident, assertive but not overly aggressive. She'll recognize his stubbornness and will not push him into a battle of wills. Instead she'll find a gentle way to work with him. She will enjoy spending time together, perhaps reading, but she will not need to spend a large quantity of time visiting or interacting with him.

TYPICAL MASTIFF MAN:

Joey's story as told by his wife, Kate:

Mastiffs were bred for war. As a defensive lineman for an NFL football team, my husband, Joey, is a modern-day warrior. During one crucial game, his warrior spirit really came through. His team was ahead by 7. The game was almost over but the ball belonged to the opponents on the ten-yard line. "Five, ten, fifty-four, hut, hut." The quarterback had the ball, faked left, dropped back, and was just short of the goal line when, against all odds, Joey tackled the guy and saved the day.

At home, it's a different ball game. My warrior likes to sleep in until noon, eat, play video games, play pool, watch TV, and wrestle with the kids. To him, a good day means not having to do much of anything. Sometimes going to a party can be too much work. At least during the season he has the games to keep him active.

This year is his last. I'm concerned about what's next, but I haven't said anything to him. We're set financially, so he doesn't have to work, and even though it may sound good to him now, I think he'll eventually get bored. A couple of days ago, he told me, "Craig, Roger, and I are going to start a sports bar/fitness center. At the bar, guys can watch a game, get all pumped up and excited, then go lift weights, shoot hoops, whatever they want, right then and there." Interesting, I thought, although the picture of some drunk guys from the bar lifting weights made me cringe. Who knows? Joey's saved the day against all odds before, why not again? The most important thing is that he's still my warrior, ready to go into battle.

FAMOUS MASTIFF MAN: Arnold Schwarzenegger as the Terminator in *Terminator 2*

A typical Mastiff warrior, the Terminator is sent to watch over and protect the boy. The ultimate bodyguard, the Terminator is big, powerful and will give his life to protect the boy. He's gentle with children and extremely loyal. He is glued to the boy and, like a true Mastiff, doesn't want to be separated from him. He is wary of strangers and will not hesitate to attack those he feels are a threat.

QUALITIES:

EXTREMELY PROTECTIVE

PREFERS A LIFE OF QUIET EASE

POWERFUL

HAS HIDDEN SENSITIVITIES

FOR EXPERIENCED WOMEN DUE TO: STUBBORNNESS AND AGGRESSIVENESS

Behavior with children:	🦴
Exercise required:	🦴🦴
Activity level:	🦴
Ease of training:	🦴🦴
Sociability with strangers:	🦴
Affection level:	🦴
Playfulness:	🦴
Protectiveness:	🦴🦴🦴
Watchdog ability:	🦴🦴🦴

PHYSICAL CHARACTERISTICS: The Rottweiler man is a large, powerfully built man whom few can ignore. Because his looks can be intimidating, most people are careful about how they approach him. His size is one thing, and on top of that, he has this look in his eyes that warns most people to take their time with him. The last thing people are tempted to do is give him a big, friendly slap on the back when they first meet.

ABILITIES & INTERESTS: Rottweiler men have many talents and are very intelligent. They're excellent at directing others. Some do this in a forceful way. Others are more laid-back. Either way, people usually find them compelling enough to do as they suggest. There are two strains of Rottweiler men. One tends to be easy-going, loving, friendly, and becomes protective only when a serious threat arises. The other strain tends to be more aggressive and will attack at the slightest provocation. Watch a Rottweiler man carefully to determine which of the two he is. Sometimes it may take a couple of years before his aggressive tendencies come out. If he starts challenging you in an aggressive manner, get help or get out. Rottweiler men, regardless of the strain, naturally excel at protection. They make great bouncers, tough law enforcement men, and powerful athletes because they are strong, tough, and intimidating. Even though most Rottweiler men are sweet, gentle men, they have the potential to scare the wits out of people. Rottweiler men love ball sports and are very athletic.

TRAINING: A Rottweiler man loves praise and attention. He thrives on it, and the more you give him praise and attention, the more he'll respond in the manner you like. Although he has a mind of his own, he responds well to firm, consistent training, because he truly wants to please his woman. Problems arise when consistency is lacking. If you're in a relationship with a Rottweiler man, be clear with him about your expectations and be consistent. Rottweiler men are natural protectors. They do not need additional encouragement to be protective. However, some women make the mistake of encouraging this behavior, and that can be dangerous. If a Rottweiler man becomes aggressive in a relationship, it is important for you to think carefully about your situation. If you have any doubts about how to handle him or the relationship, then you need either to get outside help or to get out of the relationship.

SOCIAL SKILLS: Since the Rottweiler man can be gentle and laid-back at home with his family, some women forget that he is by nature very protective. He may be distrustful of strangers, so give him time to get to know people. Most Rottweiler men who have grown up around children are great with them, especially their own. There are also Rottweiler men who are not accustomed to children, and Rottweilers may be easily annoyed by them. So if you're not certain about a Rottweiler man, watch him carefully around children, especially when he doesn't think you're watching. In a relationship with a woman, a Rottweiler may not be the most affectionate or playful of breeds. However, he can be loving and loyal. Women need to realize that even though he may appear tough, maybe even cold, he can be sensitive.

TYPE OF WOMAN: The best woman for a Rottweiler will understand his protective nature. She'll be quick with praise and resist tug-of-war arguments. Respect for his suspicious nature, including his aloofness with strangers, will make life easier. A wise woman will spend time watching a

Rottweiler man before committing to a serious relationship to make sure his temperament suits her.

TYPICAL ROTTWEILER MAN: Wes' story, as told by himself:

Years into our marriage, Rowan, my wife, told me she married me to rebel against her dad. I had to give her credit; marrying me was an excellent way to anger her father! Before our first date I showed up at their house on my Harley-Davidson motorcycle, in a Marilyn Manson T-shirt, heavy-duty boots, and pierced ear and eyebrow to get her dad's approval so I could take her to a concert. Rowan introduced us and her dad started off saying, "Two things I despise for my children. One is riding a motorcycle and two is going to a concert."

"Guess I strike out on both," I said.

"Let me ask you this," he said. "Will there be drugs at the concert you're going to?"

"Yes," I said.

"Will you be doing drugs at the concert?"

"No, I won't."

"All right," he replied. "You can take Rowan."

True to my word, I didn't do drugs at the concert, but Phil, Rowan's dad, still didn't like me. We never really understood each other. Two years later, Rowan and I married. We would do the family get-together thing because we lived in the same city, but Phil and I just stayed away from each other. We disagreed on every subject—music, politics, religion—everything. Life continued like this for another five years until one day our world turned upside down.

Rowan's mom, Trisha, worked for a company that got caught in some unscrupulous acts. Although Trisha was not involved and knew nothing about the affair, one of the top managers started pointing his finger in her direction. The media attacked. They showed up on her doorstep asking personal questions. The family was under siege. They couldn't leave the house without a reporter chasing them. After a couple of days, the family was stressed to exhaustion. When Rowan and I showed up, Trisha was on the couch crying, and Phil was looking miserable. That day the scandal had grown, and matters looked even worse for Trisha. We all knew she was innocent and would eventually be cleared, but in the meantime, life was miserable.

Furious and outraged, I walked outside. The cameras and reporters all showed up. "How long has Trisha Forrest been covering up for the company?"

"What will she do now?"

"Did Mr. Forrest know about her involvement?"

On and on the questions came until I raised my hand. "I'd like to make a statement." A hush fell. This was the first interview they had gotten from any of us. "First of all, Trisha Forrest is a fine, upstanding woman and would never be a part of the activities she has been accused of. You all are adding an incredible amount of stress to an innocent woman's life. I'm telling you all to back off and leave her alone. She will be cleared of all charges. At that time, she will speak only to those reporters she doesn't recognize from her front yard. So stick around, and you'll never get an interview. Clear off now, and your chances of an interview in the future improve dramatically. That's all." I turned around and walked back inside.

Once I was inside, Phil walked up to me. He looked into my eyes and said, "Thank you." In that moment, I knew he was saying more than just thank you. He was acknowledging our one thing in common—love of the family. We still have our differences, but it's easier now, because we know those things don't really matter.

Famous Rottweiler Man: Wesley Snipes as Blade in *Blade*

Blade, half-human half-vampire, decides to kill vampires as revenge for his mother who died at a vampire's hands. He can be loving, sensitive, and loyal to those he is close to, such as Whistler and Karen. To those he hates, such as the vampires, he is ruthless. He will do anything to protect Whistler and Karen, including risking his own life. Stubborn and independent, he lives by his rules, not anyone else's.

QUALITIES:

HAS RESCUE ABILITIES IN A TIME OF CRISIS

SLOW MOVING AND LAID-BACK

SENSITIVE, BIG, TEDDY-BEARISH MAN

ENJOYS LIFE ON HIS TERMS

FOR EXPERIENCED WOMEN DUE TO: STUBBORNNESS

Behavior with children:

Exercise required:

Activity level:

Ease of training:

Sociability with strangers:

Affection level:

Playfulness:

Protectiveness:

Watchdog ability:

PHYSICAL CHARACTERISTICS: Saint Bernard men appear large and very well grounded. If they don't get enough exercise, they can gain weight easily. These men are extremely casual and rarely get dressed up. Their version of dressed up could be another man's definition of casual. Even though they are large in size or demeanor, they are not intimidating men. Their "deep in thought" look may make them appear sad at times.

ABILITIES & INTERESTS: Saint Bernard men are strong and capable of hauling heavy loads, both physically and mentally. These men have a strong desire to aid others. They provide a strong shoulder for people who truly need assistance. Sometimes people take advantage of this, but rarely will a Saint Bernard walk away from someone in distress. Oftentimes he'll just sit and listen while someone goes on about his situation. A Saint Bernard man will do what he has to for his career, but given a choice he would prefer to take life easy and pursue interests at a leisurely pace. He is extremely laid-back, and it takes a lot to bother him; however, he can become protective if it's absolutely necessary. Exercise is something all Saint Bernard men require but don't always get. Lack of exercise can lead to weight gain and health issues.

TRAINING: A Saint Bernard man can be trained because he has a desire to please; however, he can also be stubborn. This is evident when he is doing what he wants to do and someone asks him to do something different. In that moment he may not respond, but chances are he will when he is ready. Training a Saint Bernard takes patience and understanding. Rewarding him works well, but don't make it food because he gains weight easily. Praise or activities he enjoys are best. A Saint Bernard man can take some harsh treatment, but when he's had enough he may walk, so beware.

SOCIAL SKILLS: Saint Bernard men can be friendly with new people. Usually they take their time getting to know someone. They'll study them and listen to what the other person has to say. Once they warm up to someone, they may not be overly demonstrative in their attention. The fact that they continue to interact with someone and spend time with them usually indicates their interest. Saint Bernard men like companionship and can also be independent. They will have close friends but may not need to spend a lot of time with these friends. What the relationship lacks in quantity will be made up by quality. They are excellent with children, and children love them. Saint Bernard men may not be playful like some men, but they are sturdy, safe, and loving. In a relationship, these men are very devoted and will do what they can to make a relationship work. However, some women might require more than a Saint Bernard can give.

TYPE OF WOMAN: The woman most suited for a Saint Bernard man will enjoy having a big, cuddly, teddy-bear kind of man to love. She'll understand his desire to move in the slow lane and will appreciate his compassionate nature. Exercise is something she will encourage him to do by joining him. She'll know how to work with his stubborn streak by providing lots of praise and rewards.

TYPICAL SAINT BERNARD MAN: Greg's story, as told by himself:

As a Saint Bernard, I save people. Well, more specifically, I save women. The last woman I saved left me as soon as she didn't need being saved. Some of them have lasted longer than that, but most have not. I can't seem to help myself. It's in my blood. I meet a woman in distress, and I have to help her. One woman's husband was physically abusive. Another had two children and could barely make ends meet. Then there was the longest relationship, Angie, who was trying to kill herself at a party through a drug overdose. I rushed her to the hospital and nursed her back to health. She lasted four years. But it's always the same story, just different women and slightly different circumstances.

I save them, they're grateful, and they get back on their feet. Then they become disenchanted with me, and ultimately they leave me. I'm a gentle, easygoing guy. As a financial planner, I do well enough for myself. I don't need much, and I always have enough accounts to keep me afloat. But for the women I meet, it's never good enough. They always want more and expect more from me. I know I could have a big business and make more money, but I like having free time to pursue my interests. I love to read and learn about other cultures. I travel abroad, mostly South America. I've also been to India and Africa. Anyway, this year I made a New Year's resolution. No saving women and getting into relationships. If I save them, I walk away from any other involvement.

This was easier said than done. The day of the resolution, at a friend's New Year's Eve party, this beautiful woman was crying because her boyfriend had left her that night for another woman. I sat with her and let her cry on my shoulder all night. Not only was she beautiful, she was sensitive, open, intelligent and, if I were more impetuous, I would say I was in love. When she got ready to leave, she said she'd love to get together and go out. Great! I was being tested on the first day. I thought, technically it doesn't start until tomorrow. But then I noticed that it was after midnight, so it had begun. Regretfully I told her I couldn't go out with her. I explained to her about my resolution. She was gracious and seemed to believe me.

A year went by, and I had not met any women who didn't need saving. There wasn't one available woman who was single, happy, and interested in a relationship. I started to think I was being punished for passing up the perfect chance at the New Year's Eve party. Then, one day, a woman called me, asking for some advice on her financial portfolio. We spent hours going over her books. There was an easy rapport between us. Another day our phone conversation grew into more personal matters and we found we had a lot in common. She, too, was self-employed and brought in enough to travel and enjoy her life the way she wanted to enjoy it.

The next time we spoke, I said, "Ally, would you have dinner with me this weekend?"

She said, "I would love to, Greg. I've secretly hoped you would ask me out. But what if we don't find each other attractive?"

I didn't care. I was willing to take my chances.

That Friday as I sat at the table waiting for Ally I prayed that we would be as physically attracted to each other as we were in other ways. I had just looked down at the time on my watch when I noticed a woman in a blue dress standing in front of me. I slowly raised my eyes and looked into the same gorgeous green eyes I had seen that night at the New Year's Eve party, only this time they were not filled with tears.

FAMOUS SAINT BERNARD MAN: Robin Williams as Sean McGuire in *Good Will Hunting*

Sean is a typical Saint Bernard as a therapist with a mission to help Will. Sean provides a strong arm for Will to lean on and at the same time encourages Will to find himself. Sean has the sad look of a Saint Bernard, and in this case it's because he has lost his wife. That Saint Bernard ability to sense what others cannot see is evident in his knowledge of Will's inner battles.

QUALITIES:

HARDWORKING AND FOCUSED
STRONG SENSE OF VALUES
INDEPENDENT, INTELLIGENT THINKER
PROTECTIVE IF NEED BE

FOR EXPERIENCED WOMEN DUE TO: INDEPENDENCE AND STUBBORNNESS

Behavior with children:	🦴 🦴
Exercise required:	🦴 🦴
Activity level:	🦴 🦴
Ease of training:	🦴 🦴
Sociability with strangers:	🦴
Affection level:	🦴
Playfulness:	🦴 🦴
Protectiveness:	🦴 🦴 🦴
Watchdog ability:	🦴 🦴 🦴

PHYSICAL CHARACTERISTICS: Schnauzer men have steely eyes that can cut through a person. When people meet a Schnauzer man for the first time, they feel the need to use caution. They may say he appears standoffish or possibly angry. Most Schnauzer men prefer to be neatly groomed, and the few who do not can appear rough and ragged.

ABILITIES & INTERESTS: These men can be no-nonsense hard workers. They are serious about their work and have the tenacity of terriers. They will not drop something once invested in it. Intelligent and multitalented, they can do well in many different fields. They have excellent memories and are talented problem solvers. Whatever they choose to do, they will protect it and guard it as if their lives depended on it. These men have high ideals even if they do not appear to live by all of them. They like to run the show but will take orders from those they respect. Schnauzer men enjoy playing, usually mental games such as riddles, puzzles, chess, and the like. Exercise is important for these men but sports usually don't interest them, except to occasionally watch. One-on-one or physical activities they can do by themselves work best for them.

TRAINING: A Schnauzer man knows how to pay attention and, because he is so intelligent, he can follow instructions well. However, he can be very independent and stubborn, making him a challenge. Usually, if he is approached with praise, he will do what is asked, although it may be on his schedule. If he does not respect someone or is treated harshly, he can be belligerent and uncooperative. Because of his excellent memory, he can remember any rebuke and sometimes finds it hard to let go of a grudge. Firmness is also necessary when addressing a Schnauzer man. He will be disobedient and take control if a woman cannot stand on her own. He can be feisty and tough, and at the same time he is very sensitive and can easily be hurt.

SOCIAL SKILLS: Schnauzer men are often suspicious of strangers. They can be polite but will not warm up to a person unless they feel a strong connection for and trust that person. Schnauzer men can enjoy being around others in a work or play atmosphere but are very picky about their close friends. Oftentimes their independence and ability to entertain themselves keeps them from needing close friendships. With children, they can be good but may not accept too much loud noise or rough treatment (especially of their possessions). Babies are not their strong suit. They like protecting children and being role models for them. Instilling values is important to them. In a relationship, they can be domineering unless a woman stands firm but not aggressive. With an aggressive woman, expect much discord. Schnauzer men are not overly affectionate, but if given love and respect they will return it in kind.

TYPE OF WOMAN: The woman for a Schnauzer man is strong and independent. She appreciates his brilliance, independence, and need to be protective. She will not get into a game of tug-of-war or one-upmanship with him. Instead, she will offer praise and treat him with respect. She will be comfortable with his aloofness and not need a large amount of physical affection from him.

TYPICAL SCHNAUZER MAN: Duwain's story, as told by his daughter, Jeannette:
My dad epitomizes control. He was controlling in his work, in the projects he did around the house, in the trips we took, and even in the way he related to the family. Given his out-of-control childhood—where his mother died when he was three and his father shot himself when my dad

was four, leaving him to be raised by an aunt and uncle who had an only daughter who died three years later—I think he felt the need for control. So he created it in his world.

As a "high-end" salesman, he kept impeccable records of all his clients. He always gave 100 percent to his work and was so successful, he earned multiple trips and retired at age 53. With a good sense of right and wrong and justice being served, he gave one of the trips he earned to his systems engineer and the man's wife, because my dad credited him with part of his success.

At home, my dad diligently kept the cars tuned, the yard mowed, the finances in order, and our lives on track. He didn't know what to do with us as infants, so he left that up to Mom. But as soon as we could talk, he started setting down rules, enforcing them, and instilling values in us. We probably challenged his ability to control things more than his work or Mom ever did, but for the most part, we kept in line. Sometimes if we did something beyond his control, he still made it appear that it was his plan we have that experience so we could mature and become better adults. Since my brother and I have happy, wonderful lives, I'd say Dad succeeded in guiding us. There were only two times that I remember seeing him "lose" control.

The first was when Mom went into the hospital for major surgery. The surgery required her to stay in the hospital a couple of nights, so he was home alone. When I went to visit him, I thought, what's happened? He seemed so different. He was depressed and barely said anything. Talking about Mom and the surgery, he got teary-eyed and I could tell he was genuinely afraid and worried about her. The second time was at my parents' twenty-fifth wedding anniversary party. Most of my mom's relatives were there, which included about seven aunts. As Dad made a toast, he got choked up talking about how wonderful life with my mother was and how much he loved her. I'd never seen him like this, except at funerals. To see him like this, so vulnerable in front of all these people, impressed me. I looked around the room, and most of my aunts were tearing up, and a couple of them were all-out crying.

Those moments changed my vision of my dad. Behind that controlled behavior, I now see a softer, more sensitive man. I see the dad I always wanted to have. And as I've held that new vision of him, he's become even more available to me. I understand even better why my parents' relationship has lasted 40 years. Mom has always been able to see this other side to Dad. If only I'd looked deeper, I also would have seen what was there all along.

FAMOUS SCHNAUZER MAN: William Hurt as John Robinson in *Lost In Space*

John Robinson views work as a priority—a sure sign of a Schnauzer man. While family is very important to him, he may get caught up in his work and his interests, losing track of others' needs, like not noticing his son who wants to be closer to him. John is focused, resourceful, stoic, and determined. If need be, he's a great protector but generally speaking he'll not seek out a fight. Verbal repartee, on the other hand, has an alluring quality that John can't escape. He's especially quick to argue with the pilot.

©McCARNEY/2003

QUALITIES:

CALL OF THE WILD IN HIS BLOOD

GREAT LEADER

ABLE AND WILLING TO CARRY HEAVY LOADS

EXCELLENT FAMILY MAN

FOR EXPERIENCED WOMEN DUE TO: INDEPENDENCE AND STUBBORNNESS

Behavior with children:	🦴🦴🦴
Exercise required:	🦴🦴🦴
Activity level:	🦴🦴🦴
Ease of training:	🦴
Sociability with strangers:	🦴🦴🦴
Affection level:	🦴🦴🦴
Playfulness:	🦴🦴🦴
Protectiveness:	🦴
Watchdog ability:	🦴🦴

PHYSICAL CHARACTERISTICS: Siberian Husky men are not that far removed from the wild. This shows in their very natural, untamed look, and is especially revealed in their eyes. They can conform and wear clothing styles reflecting the "norm," but when they are free to wear what they want, it can be pretty wild. They go for neatness even amidst the wild look. If they are allowed to exercise, they tend to be in decent physical shape. However, they can get so caught up in busy activities it may be difficult for them to take time to exercise.

ABILITIES & INTERESTS: Siberian Husky men are wild men at heart. They enjoy nature and need to let their hair down now and then and get crazy. These men are well equipped to haul heavy loads, not just physical, but in the form of a heavy workload. They will take on many large projects and seem to keep going when everyone around them has quit. Determination and a strong will keep them going. They can work great with a team in order to accomplish an objective. Some Husky men will push to be at the front of the pack and want to lead the rest of the team. If the other players accept him in this role, he can be a good leader. They love to be active, mentally and physically, and become bored if there is little to occupy them. Although a busy schedule makes it tough to exercise, it is very important for these men to get out and run. They can be extremely playful and enjoy games involving the mind and the physical body. Sports may or may not be their thing.

TRAINING: A Siberian Husky man is usually a challenge to train because he is intelligent, independent, and very stubborn. That wild quality that is attractive to many can become less than attractive when a Husky man does not respond to requests. If you let him off leash, you can expect he'll run off and come back only when he's good and ready. The most effective way to train a Husky man is with patience, understanding, and lots of rewards. He does very well with praise and, most important, he responds very poorly to criticism and harsh words. A Husky man will leave if treated harshly. That wild side won't allow him to stay in an abusive setting if there is any way out.

SOCIAL SKILLS: By nature, the Siberian Husky man is friendly and outgoing. While he can be gregarious when he first meets someone, he will grow bored if the conversation doesn't hold any interest for him, and he'll walk away. He is at ease and works well with others. At the same time he is very independent and can be quite content by himself. With children, he is superb. He loves children, and they love him. He can be very playful and gentle. He is not usually protective, but his family may bring out a protective streak that even he didn't know he had. In a relationship with a woman, he can be very loving, cuddly, and wild. He may have times when he pulls away and appears distant. It's just his need to connect with himself and the call of the wild.

TYPE OF WOMAN: The woman most suited for the Siberian Husky man will appreciate his wild side and embrace it. She'll be intelligent and enjoy playing with him. Life is a game to a Husky man, and she'll understand this. If a woman lets a Husky man off leash, she'll be prepared to let him go and let him return on his terms, when he's ready. Independence is an important trait for a woman who chooses a Husky man.

TYPICAL SIBERIAN HUSKY MAN: Darrel's story, as told by his wife, Felecia:
Beautiful blue eyes that penetrated my soul, a robust but not overly

muscular build, and dark, wavy, wild hair that reminded me of a gypsy—those were the qualities that first caught my attention. Later, as I stood next to him, he exuded passion; a passion for life, and I could only dream about what else. Then he spoke, and the rest of the evening was a blur. Except for the end, when he asked for my number and left the party.

Two days later, he called and asked me out. We went on a picnic in the mountains. He liked to mountain-climb and brought gear for us. I thought he was crazy, but I trusted him and let him attach all the ropes, assuring me that he wouldn't let anything happen to me. At one point in the climb, I lost my footing and fell. I didn't fall far, but I started praying, thinking this was it, the end, when *snap,* the line went tight and Darrel had the line secured. "It's okay, Felecia, I've got you and I'm not letting go." When we were back on the ground I knew I could spend the rest of my life with this man. There was only one catch—he was nowhere near being able to commit to one person in a relationship. With profound sadness, I accepted this fact. We went out occasionally, and every time we had the best time!

One day I was offered a great job opportunity in a new city, so I took it. I told Darrel I was leaving and asked him to visit. He didn't visit but we got in touch a couple of times a year. After about three years, I went back to attend a friend's wedding and, while I was there, I spent the weekend with Darrel. Everything was still the same between us, including his need for freedom.

During those first three years and the ones following, I dated other people and some of them were great guys, but none of them left me with that sense of "He's the one." I wasn't concerned about finding a man. Yes, I wanted to get married and have a family, but I didn't want to settle for a relationship that wasn't right for me.

For another three years, Darrel and I would talk and catch up. I'd listen to his adventures as a photographer and lecturer, and he'd listen to my stories about being a graphic designer. Occasionally we would see each other and have time to catch up in person. Then, one day, Darrel said he was coming to town and wanted to talk to me about something very important. When he arrived, he said, "Felecia, you know you are the only woman

I've ever really loved. I'm torn. On the one hand, I want my freedom, adventure, the ability to live my life the way I want to live it. On the other hand, I want a family. I don't know how to have both. But if it's possible to do it, I think I could do it with you. What do you think?"

I smiled, "I think we could do it. I don't know how either. We'll just have to make it up as we go along. We'll treat it like a grand adventure." So we did just that. We agreed from the start to honor each other. That meant maintaining our independence and yet creating a family that was united in love. I'll admit I had my suspicions about Darrel being able to stay committed, but what's the worst that could happen? We have children, get divorced, and I'm a single parent. Well, that all sounded pretty horrible to me, but if I didn't try I might be throwing away the best chance for happiness I could ever have with a man.

As soon as we had our first daughter, I knew he would never leave. His commitment to me and our family keeps me in awe. Every day, I am grateful for another day with this Husky man. Life continues to be an adventure. Even when we're apart, I feel there's a lifeline connecting us to one another—just in case the other falls, like that first date on the mountain.

FAMOUS SIBERIAN HUSKY MAN: Harrison Ford as Indiana Jones in *Raiders of the Lost Ark*

Indiana Jones needs freedom. While he can teach as a professor, he craves adventure. Adventure, for him, may be extreme for most Siberian Husky men, but all Husky men long for some element of daring in their lives. Indiana can be loving and devoted, especially if he's not kept on too short a leash. In the first movie, he'll risk anything to rescue his "love interest." He prefers being in the lead, the first to find the treasure. He'll carry the extra load and go the extra mile to save the world.

9

THE TERRIER GROUP

THE TERRIER GROUP of men have in common playfulness, tenacity, spunk, and disdain for people who lack integrity. They can be very stubborn and will not give up easily.

AIREDALE TERRIER: These guys are bouncy clowns in big bodies. For every bit of love they give, they give an equal amount of mischief.

AMERICAN STAFFORDSHIRE TERRIER OR PIT BULL: These rugged-looking guys can scare most people with one glance. But when their playful side comes out you'll wonder why you were ever afraid.

BULL TERRIER: These strong-willed but loving guys enjoy a good debate. If you say the sky is blue, they'll say it's purple.

MINIATURE SCHNAUZER: These busy guys are the most fun-loving of the Schnauzers. They have a great sense of humor and can get a little feisty in a playful way.

PARSON (JACK) RUSSELL TERRIER: These guys are the cutest, most entertaining tornados you will ever meet. You will never be bored with a man like this.

SCOTTISH TERRIER: These stoic and independent guys can be very sophisticated or very carefree. It depends on their mood. Watch for nipping and barking.

WEST HIGHLAND WHITE TERRIER: These people-loving guys can be lots of fun. They're less aggressive than other terrier men but still a bit feisty . . . in a cute way.

McCartney/2003

QUALITIES:

Has many interests

Enjoys adventure

Mischievous sense of humor

Playfully stubborn

FOR EXPERIENCED WOMEN DUE TO: STUBBORNNESS

Behavior with children:

Exercise required:

Activity level:

Ease of training:

Sociability with strangers:

Affection level:

Playfulness:

Protectiveness:

Watchdog ability:

PHYSICAL CHARACTERISTICS: Airedale Terrier men have wiry hair, and you will often find one sporting a goatee, which makes him look distinguished. Airedale men are the most robust men in the Terrier group. They're large and sturdy men. Their dress reflects a love of the outdoors; they're into casual, comfortable, and practical.

ABILITIES & INTERESTS: Airedale Terrier men are extremely talented and versatile. Whatever they apply themselves to, they can do. And it may change from day to day because they are easily bored. Airedale men work well in the police force as detectives because they enjoy hunting criminals. They have a second nature of sniffing out their prey. Investigative work also suits them. Some Airedale men enjoy outdoor game hunting as well. They can be mischievous and they love to clown around. Keeping the fun and games going is their forte. Airedale men love the outdoors, and they especially love water sports such as surfing, swimming, waterskiing, and fishing.

TRAINING: An Airedale Terrier man can be a challenge because he holds onto his puppy ways and will use his boyish charm and mischievous spirit to get his way. The best way to approach an Airedale man is with lots of praise and rewards. One reward that works well is laughing at his jokes and appreciating his sense of humor, when it is funny, and appropriate. If not, then ignore him—do not belittle him, especially in front of others. He can be stubborn, so be careful of the tug-of-war game.

SOCIAL SKILLS:
Airedale Terrier men are naturals in social settings. The saying "they've never met a stranger" holds true for them. People immediately feel at ease with them, even if they find the Airedale man a little quirky. Airedale men are gregarious and friendly when they first meet someone, but if their interest is not kept, they'll quickly move on to the next person. Airedale men can be fun family men, but don't expect them to be overly involved in the early lives of the children. In a loving relationship, Airedale men are very devoted and loving. They can be challenging at times because of their stubborn natures, but you can count on them to be there when you need them.

TYPE OF WOMAN:
A woman with a great sense of humor will work best with an Airedale Terrier man. She must accept his eccentric nature and his mischievous ways. When he becomes stubborn and hardheaded, she'll need patience. She'll understand how to work with him and not get dragged into a game of tug-of-war. A love of the outdoors would also help.

TYPICAL AIREDALE TERRIER MAN:
Kent's story, as told by his cousin:

Through the years, Kent's passions have changed. For a while, he was devoted to living on the beach and surfing, then to building a house, then to doing massage work, and then to traveling to mines and collecting crystals along with other rocks and semiprecious stones. Most recently, his passion has been wildlife photography.

The owners of a big spread of land allowed him access for photography, and on one expedition he felt like the Crocodile Hunter in an all-out adventure worthy of being televised. It started when he saw a raccoon. Being downwind, he started taking photos. Then he put some food out to tempt the raccoon into giving him some better shots. When he got ready to leave, the raccoon ran after him. It became extremely pushy and even tried to grab his leg. Because the raccoon became so aggressive, Kent thought about the threat of rabies and decided to hightail it out of there. A little while later he came upon some wild pigs. Again, he started taking some shots from downwind. All at once, the pigs saw him and charged. You might think pigs charging you would be no big deal, but wild pigs can be dangerous. Despite his fear, there wasn't much Kent could do out there in the open, so he stood his ground and eventually, after a few charges, they left him alone.

A few minutes later, he stepped over what appeared to be a stick but in reality was a rattlesnake. As he jumped high in the air, it barely missed him and again he took off running. After resting for a moment, he decided to photograph some marsh birds. Coming upon a swampy area, he waded into the water to see what he could find. About halfway through, with water up to his thighs, he saw an alligator on the bank. Great, he thought. Alligators! Hoping that was the only one in the area, he pushed through the swamp as fast as he could.

The next day at work, where he does body-work therapy on children with various disabilities, he felt relief at having made it through the previous day unscathed. Working on one of the children a little while later, he was suddenly shocked to realize that this child had his arm in his mouth. And he wasn't playing around. He was clamped down hard. It took what seemed like hours to pry the child off Kent.

Kent always enjoys a good joke, and this was one divine joke that Kent could appreciate. He had escaped his harrowing adventures in the wild only to be bitten by a child at work.

FAMOUS AIREDALE TERRIER MAN: Kramer on *Seinfeld*

Kramer is the Airedale clown. As soon as he walks in the door you want to laugh, but his humor may be at his friend's expense. He's a handful for any woman. Perhaps that's why he's remained a bachelor for so long. He has friends, but his social skills are unconventional. When he first meets someone, he can be buddy-buddy until he's ready to do something else, and then he's on to the next person or thing.

McCartney/2003

QUALITIES:

FEISTY AND TOUGH

REBELLIOUS, GOES AGAINST OTHERS FOR JUSTICE

EXTREMELY PROTECTIVE

CARING, WARM HEART UNDER A TOUGH FACADE

FOR EXPERIENCED WOMEN DUE TO: STUBBORNNESS AND AGGRESSIVENESS	
Behavior with children:	🦴
Exercise required:	🦴 🦴
Activity level:	🦴 🦴 🦴
Ease of training:	🦴
Sociability with strangers:	🦴 🦴
Affection level:	🦴 🦴
Playfulness:	🦴 🦴
Protectiveness:	🦴 🦴 🦴
Watchdog ability:	🦴 🦴 🦴

PHYSICAL CHARACTERISTICS: American Staffordshire Terrier men, also known as Pit Bull men look tough. Based on appearances, they could play the roles of Mafiosi gang members and fighters. Most Pit Bull men puff out their chests and strut their stuff. Pit Bull men have very muscular physiques, and although they may gain weight, there will always be solid muscle under the fat.

ABILITIES & INTERESTS: Pit Bull men by nature are fighters. They'll stand up to anyone or anything that gets in their way. They can also be very gentle and loving. They have received a bad rap because some have viciously attacked other people and animals. A balanced Pit Bull will know when standing up for oneself or for loved ones is appropriate and when it is not. Pit Bull men make excellent rebels. They'll bravely stand up against injustice and fight for what they think is right. Pit Bull men do not concern themselves with what others think about them, so they are prepared to go against the "norm" and stand up for what they believe in. They do, however, care about the opinions of those they love, even if they pretend not to. A career that some Pit Bull men excel in is law. As lawyers, they can go for the jugular of a witness on the stand and have that witness contradicting himself because he's so nervous. Few people can keep their cool and fight off a Pit Bull man at their throats. Pit Bull men love physical activity and sports. It's finding time for these activities in the midst of their busy schedules that is the challenge.

TRAINING: A Pit Bull man may not be easy to train. He will be stubborn and try his best to get the upper hand. Be firm and steady with him and give him lots of praise. Never be competitive with a Pit Bull man. In a game of tug-of-war, he will do anything to win. And absolutely under no circumstances should you hit a Pit Bull man, or you are asking for trouble. Pay attention to how he was raised and what kind of relationship he had with his mother. This will tell you much about how he will respond to the woman in his life. While this is true of all breeds, it is especially important with a Pit Bull man. If conflicts arise in the relationship and he shows signs of aggression, get professional help.

SOCIAL SKILLS: Pit Bull men can be civil to strangers, but they won't rush up to meet a new person, and they won't waste their time trying to dazzle someone they don't know. They are particular about whom they associate with. You may wonder about their choice of friends sometimes, because they're apt to be tough men. A Pit Bull has little use for someone he considers a "softie." Give him a buddy he can trust to back him up in a fight. Be prepared for his combative nature to come forth. He may become combative at a party with a stranger or a good friend he's known for years. You never know when this aggressive side may show itself. Despite their tough façade, they are very sensitive to any type of abuse. Some Pit Bull men can make excellent fathers, especially if they grew up around children and like children. I also know Pit Bull men who are great with other people's children but rough with their own. If a Pit Bull man is good with his children, he can be extremely devoted and protective of them. In a relationship, these men can be playful and affectionate, but not overly so. They have a tendency to be very protective and can become jealous.

TYPE OF WOMAN: The best woman for a Pit Bull man is very self-confident and resilient. She's not easily intimidated. She is extremely loving and compassionate, and she understands that there are times to let him win, or at least think he has won. She's not so caught up in her own ego that she has to be right. She knows when and how to back out of a fight. She understands and respects his need to be tough and his need to stand up for what he believes in.

TYPICAL AMERICAN PIT BULL MAN: Roy's story, as told by his sister, Lue:

Well, what can I say? My brother Roy is a special character. Some would call him a "hell raiser," but inside that tough outer coating is a very sensitive and caring guy. I'll tell you how I know that.

Roy is two years older than I, so we grew up very close to each other, but it seemed he blazed his own trail. He was always getting into trouble. He did crazy stuff like jumping off the roof into the pool, biting doves' heads off to kill them when we were dove hunting, and so much more.

He never wanted me to date any of his friends in school. I always thought it was because he just thought it would be uncool for his sister to date his friends. Later in life, he told me they were never good enough.

One time when I was a freshman, Roy really came through for me. It was a tradition at my school to initiate some of the freshmen by taking them to the cemetery and stripping them and tying them to the tombstones. I was scared to death, and talk was going around that it was going to happen after the football game one night. Some senior girls grabbed me and some of my girlfriends and threw us in the back of a pickup truck. The girls sat on us to keep us from jumping out. I was screaming for help when Roy saw me.

He jumped in his truck with one of his friends and followed the truck I was in. He lost me at the cemetery. Meanwhile, two girls were trying to get my shirt off. I broke away and started running with my shirt half off. Suddenly, Roy appeared with his truck out of nowhere. "Get in!" he yelled, and some friends and I jumped in.

The next day I heard the horror stories of people being taped to tombstones and being scared. He was like a knight in shining armor coming to my rescue.

FAMOUS AMERICAN PIT BULL MAN: Joe Pesci as Vincent LaGuardia Gambino in *My Cousin Vinny*

Vincent is a tough Pit Bull. He's also a devoted family man. When his cousin gets in trouble, Vinny's there to get him out. As a lawyer, he's ruthless. He doesn't let anything stand in his way. He's extremely stubborn and continues to cause problems in the courtroom, so much so that he's found in contempt of court more than once. Tough with everyone else, he's sensitive to criticism by his equally tough and sassy girlfriend, Mona.

QUALITIES:

    TENACIOUS ABILITY TO HOLD ON TO THINGS

    EXCELLENT DEBATERS

    POSSESS A SIXTH SENSE ABOUT PEOPLE

    HAVE STRONG ETHICS

FOR EXPERIENCED WOMEN DUE TO: INDEPENDENCE AND STUBBORNNESS

Behavior with children:

Exercise required:

Activity level:

Ease of training:

Sociability with strangers:

Affection level:

Playfulness:

Protectiveness:

Watchdog ability:

PHYSICAL CHARACTERISTICS: Bull Terrier men can appear tough with a swagger to their walk, but it's mostly for show. They are particular about their dress, being very tidy, and they prefer casual to suit and tie. These men are very alert and watchful. They seem to study every move and every word spoken.

ABILITIES & INTERESTS: The Bull Terrier man is very watchful and has a desire to protect; however, he isn't overly protective and will fight only when there are no more options left. He can be argumentative and play devil's advocate, which he is good at because he is so clever. But when push comes to shove, he'll usually walk away. With the tenaciousness of most terriers, he can take hold of something and not let go until he's good and ready. This is especially true of projects, ideas, and beliefs. He has issues with people who lack integrity, because he works hard to live his life by high ideals. Not that he always succeeds, but he does his best. These men are mischievous, clever, and intelligent, and they need mental stimulation or they grow bored and can become destructive. Physical exercise is also important for these men. Organized sports may not be their thing, although they can work well with others. Usually, they prefer exercise they can do alone like jogging, weights, tai chi, etc.

TRAINING: Training a Bull Terrier man can be fun and rewarding, if you know how to approach him and you have infinite patience. He's very quick and understands what you want; however, he can be extremely stubborn. If he's busy with something else, or if your request turns into a battle of wills, he may dig his heels in and refuse to budge. Often the best approach to less-than-excellent behavior is to ignore him. Praise and rewards work well, although it may take a lot of both. Incorporating play into training is especially effective. A Bull Terrier man can also be independent, which makes him more challenging. Expect him to put things off until he's ready, and allow him the freedom to sometimes say no.

SOCIAL SKILLS:
Bull Terrier men can be polite, but they certainly take their time before they warm up to strangers. Friendships with Bull Terriers can be interesting. They appreciate discussions, especially with people as clever as themselves. And when these discussions turn heated, they often enjoy them even more. They especially love to interrogate people. It's not that they are trying to be difficult. It's just that this type of banter is mentally stimulating and interesting for them. They can be good with children, although they are best with older children. Children generally enjoy them, but the Bull Terrier's tough attitude can be intimidating to some children. These men tend to be very protective of their children. In a relationship, they are loyal and enjoy spending quality time with those they love. They will want a partner with whom they can play and have fun.

TYPE OF WOMAN:
The best woman for a Bull Terrier man will enjoy playing and will appreciate his clever yet mischievous ways. She'll accept and perhaps even enjoy his love for heavy, heated discussions. If not, she'll know how to defuse him when he tries it with her. She will instead encourage him to find friends who appreciate his quick repartee. Obedience will not matter much to her; she'll be independent enough to take care of herself.

TYPICAL BULL TERRIER MAN:
Todd's story, as told by a friend, Sarah:

As a receptionist, I am always the first person to greet people when they come into the office. Many of our patients come every week, so, over time, I get to know them fairly well. Todd is quite a character. When he first started coming in, I noticed that if I said it was a beautiful day, he would come back with, "What makes it beautiful, just because it's sunny?

Maybe it would be more beautiful if it were cloudy."

Or if I said, "I like your tie, Todd," he'd say, "I don't. I only wear it when my mother-in-law visits, since she gave it to me."

Or sports comments such as, "Todd, did you watch the basketball game last night? The Lakers were amazing, outscoring their opponents by 26 points!"

"It was okay. I thought they could have done better."

Over time I learned to just smile say, "Hi, Todd, you can go in," and leave it at that. I'll have to admit that I admired and respected his way of playing devil's advocate. It's just that most of the time, I didn't want to play the game at the office in front of others. He was never rude or mean about it, just opinionated and sometimes even playful. If I ever took the bait and replied, he had the ability to hold on and not let go. In a game of verbal tug-of-war, I knew I could never win.

On a busy night, with the reception area packed with people, a patient named Jake came into the office. This patient was having a challenging day and decided to direct it at me. He waved his hands in the air, yelling at and berating me. I was stupefied. I had no idea what he was yelling about. While I sat there stunned, Todd walked up and sternly told the man, "I think you need to cool off, sir. Sarah doesn't deserve this. If you have a problem, I suggest you relax first, then talk to her . . . calmly."

Jake stormed off. The next day, he was able to approach me peacefully and apologize. I was grateful to Todd for his ability to stand up to this man without escalating the conflict. It would have been easy for Todd to do nothing or to be verbally abusive back to the man. I have a new respect for Todd and feel fortunate to have a Bull Terrier man as a friend.

Famous Bull Terrier Man: Kevin Costner as Crash Davis in *Bull Durham*

Crash Davis, intelligent and baseball-savvy, is nonetheless on his way out of the minor league because of his age. He's kept on mainly to help instruct the new up-and-coming players. He is opinionated and lets everyone know what he thinks. Most of the time his contrary ways come out verbally, but every now and then, he's willing to go head-to-head and fight for his beliefs. Annie faces her biggest challenge and closest equal when she meets Crash. Few men can stand up to her and appreciate her feisty, passionate, and intellectual ways as Crash does.

©McCartney/2003

QUALITIES:

INTELLIGENT AND DRIVEN

LOVINGLY PLAYFUL

STRONG VALUES

FEISTY IN A FUN WAY

FINE FOR NOVICE WOMEN

Behavior with children:

Exercise required:

Activity level:

Ease of training:

Sociability with strangers:

Affection level:

Playfulness:

Protectiveness:

Watchdog ability:

PHYSICAL CHARACTERISTICS: The Miniature Schnauzer man is similar in appearance to the Working Group Schnauzer, only he appears less intimidating. He may or may not be smaller in size. He has a charming grin that puts most people at ease. He can also be particular about his appearance, looking quite distinguished, and, when he isn't concerned, he can look somewhat disheveled.

ABILITIES & INTERESTS: The Mini Schnauzer, like other Terriers, has a radar that easily and effectively locates suspicious people and situations. They are tenacious in their quest for justice. Integrity is very important to them, and they work hard to live in alignment with their principles. These men tend to be a bit more laid-back than most Terrier men; however, compared to some of the other breeds of men, they may not appear very relaxed. Mini Schnauzer men are very comical and playful. They can keep people entertained with their cute antics. Companionship is important to these men, and they will have a strong desire to spend quality time with those they love. Exercise is a good idea, but they do not require or necessarily desire much.

TRAINING: A Mini Schnauzer man is fairly easy to train because he pays attention and is intelligent. Still, being a Terrier, he can be independent and scrappy. He may call upon his cute ways to avoid confrontation and trouble. Most of the time this will work, but you must be willing to ignore him when this behavior is inappropriate. Praise is nice, and rewards work even better. If you are giving of your time, you will find him easier to control. His sweet disposition and playful nature make training a real joy. You must understand that the Mini Schnauzer may complain about having to do something and this could take the form of a comical complaint or whininess. Eventually, he will do what is asked of him, most of the time.

SOCIAL SKILLS:
The Mini Schnauzer man may be cautious with strangers at first due to his suspicious nature. He's so proficient at picking up on negative vibes that he can usually assess the quality of a person within a short amount of time. He enjoys having a group of friends and can be extremely playful when he's comfortable. He's so amiable that most people easily accept him into their circles. He works well with others and enjoys following them more than leading. With children, the Mini Schnauzer can be good as long as the children are older. Screaming babies may not interest him. He enjoys playing with children, but doesn't enjoy too much rough play. In a relationship, he can be very attentive. He may even become so attached he won't want to leave a woman's side.

TYPE OF WOMAN:
The woman most suited for a Mini Schnauzer will appreciate the high degree of integrity that he lives by. She'll recognize his sixth sense about people and situations, and she will respect his opinions on such matters. Having him close by her side will delight her. She knows he may not always respond immediately, but he'll do what's needed eventually.

TYPICAL MINIATURE SCHNAUZER MAN:
Alex's story, as told by his wife, Carol:

Can love follow you for five years, be right under your nose, and you not see it? It happened to me. Alex and I were great friends starting in high school, when we were in a play together. I played Juliet, but he was no Romeo. Romeo was this gorgeous blond guy, Hugh, with dreamy blue eyes. Alex was the shy, quiet guy in the back with glasses. What Alex lacked in looks he made up for in genuine sweetness. When I wanted to rehearse my lines or practice a scene, he was always there. Looking back, I was blind not to see love written all over his face every time he looked at me. I was too caught up in Hugh.

Hugh didn't work out, but Alex and I remained friends, and over the years our friendship grew. We went off to college together where I studied theater arts and Alex pursued an education in computer programming. Being so intelligent, he did exceedingly well in all his classes. Gentle, loving Alex was there with a handkerchief after every one of my failed relationships. He helped me eat a gallon of Blue Bell ice cream when I didn't get a part in *West Side Story*. I can't think of high school or college without thinking of Alex's part in it.

Our fourth year in college, I had the lead role as Dulcinea in *Man of La Mancha*. For me, this was big time. My chance to shine. I skipped meals, classes, anything to rehearse my lines. Two nights before the first performance, I couldn't sleep. I asked Alex, late at night, to help me go through my lines for the hundredth time. In this particular scene, Don Quixote kisses Dulcinea, lightly on the lips. We'd never practiced a kiss before, but I wanted it to be perfect, so Alex kissed me. It was the briefest of kisses. If the earth was a representation of the amount of time Alex and I had spent together, that kiss was the size of a heart— so small and yet so amazingly powerful! That night, lying in bed, I still felt his lips on mine. The next day, they were still there. Opening night, they still lingered. I wrote it off to nerves. I was just excited, right? I mean Alex was sweet and dear to me. But I was usually attracted to flashier men. Alex was very accomplished, lively, and fun, but he could easily blend into the background.

The performances were outstanding, the play was over, and still I felt Alex's lips on mine, and I saw his face inches from mine and I wanted more. I felt the only way to assure myself was to kiss him again and see if it was real. Walking with Alex on campus, at night, back from the library, I stopped and turned to face him. He was talking about the future using computer technology when, mid-sentence, I kissed him. It was a slow, gentle, lingering kiss. That kiss transformed my best friend into more than just a best friend. What he had known for five years, and what he had held onto with Terrier tenacity, became my reality as well . . . we loved each other.

FAMOUS MINIATURE SCHNAUZER MAN: Ben Stiller as Rabbi Jacob Schram in *Keeping the Faith*

Rabbi Jacob, with Terrier feistiness, stirs things up in the temple. He even brings gospel singers in to liven things up. All the mothers try to set their daughters up with him because he's such a sweet, upstanding, good man. He has high standards and refuses to settle for just any woman.

QUALITIES:

HAPPY, CHEERFUL DISPOSITION

STRONG DESIRE FOR A PLAYFUL PARTNER

"GO FOR IT" ATTITUDE ABOUT LIFE

FUN TORNADO

FINE FOR NOVICE WOMEN

Behavior with children:	🦴🦴
Exercise required:	🦴🦴
Activity level:	🦴🦴🦴
Ease of training:	🦴
Sociability with strangers:	🦴🦴
Affection level:	🦴🦴
Playfulness:	🦴🦴🦴
Protectiveness:	🦴
Watchdog ability:	🦴🦴🦴

PHYSICAL CHARACTERISTICS: Formerly referred to as Jack Russell Terriers, now known as Parson Russell Terriers, these fastidious men are particular about their appearance and are neatly dressed regardless of where they are going or what they are doing. You won't find a Parson Russell jogging in old sweat pants with holes in them unless it's "in style." They are well groomed, usually sporting a short, neatly trimmed hairstyle. Aside from his dress, you can also spot a Parson Russell Terrier man by his demeanor. He carries himself with pride, and he'll puff his chest out and give a little swagger to his walk to show you he's hot stuff. He looks cute when he does it, though, not tough like some breeds.

ABILITIES & INTERESTS: Cute and playful, the Parson Russell Terrier man is also bold, brash, and high-spirited. One minute you'll think he's so adorable and cuddly. The next you may wonder if a tornado just entered his body because he's on a tear about something and leaves chaos in his wake. He's an expert at trouble. His adventures will lead him into exciting situations and some very tight spots. Don't be surprised if you have to come to his rescue. His main objective is to expose vermin. He'll sniff out the rats and go after them with a vengeance. Parson Russell men cannot abide people who lack integrity. Not to say they always demonstrate integrity, but they are working on their own as well as everyone else's.

Parson Russell Terrier men need to stay busy and will fill their time with many projects. Keep a Parson Russell Terrier busy and he'll make a great partner. If he's bored, he may bark at you. It's his way of communicating, "Let's do something!" He'll also bark when he becomes overly excited. Parson Russell Terrier men enjoy exercise if it's fun, especially in the company of others. Sometimes their busy lifestyle interferes with exercise.

TRAINING: The Parson Russell Terrier man may be difficult to train since he's impulsive and somewhat self-involved. He doesn't mean to be difficult; he just lives life by his own rules. When you ask a Parson Russell to do something, you can expect him to oblige only when it's convenient for him. Although training is challenging and close to impossible, it doesn't need to be if you incorporate the appropriate reward. Every man has a tender spot. Find that spot, and he'll be more eager to please. Verbal praise will always win a Parson Russell Terrier over. Since Parson Russells love to play, you'll find training easier when you incorporate play. Ball sports are a big hit.

SOCIAL SKILLS: A Parson Russell Terrier man can win his way into almost anyone's heart with his charm and unpretentious ways, but he's picky about the company he keeps. And he does not tolerate people who lack integrity. A Parson Russell Terrier man will have a strong circle of people he loves and trusts. He has a strong desire to be with people and prefers not being alone. Toddlers are not his specialty. He can be around them and be trusted with them, but when they start to scream, you'll probably find him walking out the door. If you marry a Parson Russell and want to have children, be prepared to be the primary caretaker until they are older. Then he'll possibly step in and lend a hand. In a relationship, he will be extremely playful, more than most women can handle. Showering a woman with gifts and affection makes him happy. He'll enjoy a woman by his side, one who can keep up with him.

TYPE OF WOMAN: The woman for a Parson Russell Terrier man is playful, enjoys adventure, and even a little mischief. She realizes he has a lot of energy and rarely slows down. She rewards him by praising him and stroking his tender spots. She realizes he hates to be alone and that he loves to spend time with her and with friends.

TYPICAL PARSON RUSSELL TERRIER MAN: Bryan's story, as told by himself:

When I was a little boy, I was so happy I would start singing or whistling at the breakfast table or dinner table. But not too far into my fun celebrating feeling good, one of my parents would break away from their conversation and scold me for my behavior. At school, this abundance of happy energy led to "C's" in conduct, which led to a belt whipping at home. So I learned to hide some of the happy feelings. In my teens, discovering girls, I found it hard to hide this joy and happiness. At a party or a dance, I was the hit of the event, and people would say, "We can't start the party until you arrive." Of course I always arrived late, because Dad believed ranch work was far more important than anything related to fun. When I found a pretty girl to take out, I had a problem being too happy all the time. And, as one girl said, "Bryan, you're just too nice." A later relationship, which lasted a while, was even more frustrating. She resented my happiness and I again found myself suppressing my joy. We broke up.

After many years and many dates, I resigned myself to the idea that I was so happy whistling when I awoke and singing in the shower that I would live my life alone rather than pretending to be somebody else. This was the last thing I ever thought I would decide to do, because I thought I would find my soul mate. Someone who would be happy with herself, be easy to please, and be supportive of my happy nature. Still, I was hopeful about finding this soul mate . . . someday.

At about 46 years of age, after much prayer and even a Moon Dance ceremony with the American Indians, where I did not eat or drink for three days, I had failed to find this woman. Then one day, I noticed a redhead named Charise who worked in the area where I worked. In the couple of years I had known her, I realized Charise always seemed happy. At an event one evening, I asked her to help me out in a situation, and she replied, "I would, but I'm not dressed for this event you speak of."

"No problem," I replied. "Let's go shopping."

Six dates and lots of laughter later, we kissed at the beach, and, as they say, the rest is history. We've been happily married for seven years. Charise enjoys and honors my playful, happy, boisterous nature. What a lucky man I am!

FAMOUS PARSON RUSSELL TERRIER MAN: Leonardo Di Caprio as Jack Dawson in *Titanic*

Jack is a Parson Russell Terrier at its finest. He's adventurous and has enough energy for everyone on the *Titanic*. Rose's fiancée is pegged as untrustworthy, and Jack does his best to reveal that characteristic to Rose. Jack's clever ways and boyish charm enchant everyone he meets, except those who should not be trusted. Jack, proud of who he is, doesn't buy into the class divisions idea. He believes that he and Rose are equals, regardless of his upbringing and his lack of money.

THE SCOTTISH TERRIER MAN

QUALITIES:

TENACIOUS

STANDS UP FOR INTEGRITY

INDEPENDENT AND FEISTY

EXTREMELY LOYAL AND DEPENDABLE

FINE FOR NOVICE WOMEN

Behavior with children:

Exercise required:

Activity level:

Ease of training:

Sociability with strangers:

Affection level:

Playfulness:

Protectiveness:

Watchdog ability:

PHYSICAL CHARACTERISTICS: Scottish Terrier men are rugged, distinguished-looking men. Some people might say they appear pompous, and they can be. They prefer wearing beards and look good in them. Their facial hair may take over their faces unless they keep it trimmed. Checkered patterns, especially red, look stunning on these men. They tend to be upscale casual in their dress. They often have a mischievous look on their faces that amuses people and makes them wonder what they know.

ABILITIES & INTERESTS: Scottish Terrier men are tough guys who will challenge anyone and will sometimes take on more than they can handle. Once they throw themselves into something, they rarely back down. Like most Terriers, they have a nose for sniffing out vermin and have issues with people who cannot be trusted. They may dedicate themselves to righting social situations that they feel are unfair or unjust. Give them a cause and they are excellent crusaders. Scottish Terrier men don't always follow instructions because they tend to be slightly independent. Self-employment situations or work environments that give them a lot of leeway work best for them. These men love adventure and love to travel. Careers where they can be on the road may appeal to them. Exercise is beneficial, but they don't require a lot. Generally they enjoy working out at the gym or getting outside and jogging. They also enjoy some sports.

TRAINING: Training a Scottish Terrier man can be extremely challenging. He is mildly independent and stubborn. However, he is so cute when being disobedient that it is hard to stay mad at him. When he is focused, it may be impossible to get his attention. Yelling certainly doesn't work. Occasionally, a treat will work. The best way to work with a Scotty man is to incorporate play. If you disguise work as play, he may fall for it and actually enjoy it. Of course, that won't work all the time, so there may be times when you have to let him have his way while you find some other way to get things done. Letting him occasionally say no without getting in trouble will make him more willing to say yes.

SOCIAL SKILLS: Scotty men are not the friendliest when meeting someone for the first time. They aren't rude; they just appear uninterested unless there's something in it for them. Suspicious by nature, they'll study someone and quickly know whether or not to trust them. Scotties do not need many friends, but they appreciate one or two close friendships. Once they've become friends with someone, they can be incredibly loyal and trustworthy. In a work environment they can be cooperative, but if they disagree, they can put up a good fight and skillfully argue their point. They can be good fathers as children get older. Setting an example is important to them, and they will teach their children values. Playtime with children is something they enjoy, although they may get a little too feisty. In a relationship, they are extremely loyal, rarely noticing anyone else. They can be very affectionate and tender. Just don't expect them to be at your beck and call all the time.

TYPE OF WOMAN: The woman most suited for a Scottish Terrier man will appreciate his tough, tenacious quest for justice and his desire to right wrongs. She'll get a kick out of his comical, spunky attitude. She will be independent like him and at the same time enjoy spending quality time together focusing on each other. Whether or not he does what she asks will be okay with her, and she'll put forth the effort to make chores and other tasks playful and fun.

TYPICAL SCOTTISH TERRIER MAN: Will's story, as told by himself:

You'll have a hard time finding me. First you have to traverse four miles of dirt road, and most of that is swampy marshland. If you don't know what you're doing and where you're going, you'll end up stuck in the mud. If you make it through that, you still won't see our house. It's hidden behind trees, vines, and brush. But I can see you. I know where the holes are in the vines. I keep them open so I'll know who's coming to visit. Not that we get many visitors.

We mainly keep to ourselves when we're home. I work as a guard at the local prison. I'm in one of the top towers where I can keep an eye on the yard below. I've never had to use my abilities at the prison, but I'm a marksman. I do target practice behind our house. One night while I was taking some shots, I saw this large pickup truck go by with about five 50 gallon drums (big plastic containers). It was odd to see anyone driving out here, but I went back to shooting. A couple of weeks later, I saw the same truck go by with another five drums in it. Very strange. What's in the drums? I wondered.

I kept my eyes open, and again, after a couple of weeks they came driving by. I jumped in my car, thinking I better follow these guys and see what they're up to. I didn't want to spook them, so I didn't get too close. All of a sudden, two of my tires blew out. POW! POW! The car swerved back and forth over the dirt road and then slammed into a huge tree right by the road. I don't know how long I lay there—hours, probably. A distant neighbor happened to see me as he drove home and called an ambulance. When I came to, there was a policeman waiting for me. "Your tires had spikes in them that we suspect were deliberately placed in the road. Your neighbor was lucky he didn't pick any up in his tires. But the ambulance got one. Do you have any idea who would have thrown those down?"

I told him about the pickup I was following, and he said he'd check it out. A couple of weeks later, the policeman called. "We got them. Turns out these two guys were dumping chemicals from a small manufacturing plant. The company denies knowledge of it, claiming they paid the guys for "proper" disposal. But we got the two men, and they're facing some heavy fines for illegal dumping. What's more, we found spikes in their pickup truck, like the ones in your tires. And that's gonna get them some time. Who knows, you might just get to watch these guys from your tower at the prison!"

Justice was served, and I rest easy knowing I played some small role in protecting this swamp I call home.

FAMOUS SCOTTISH TERRIER MAN: James Doohan as Scotty on *Star Trek*

Scotty is the engineer aboard the Starship Enterprise. As the engineer, he ferrets out the problems in the system. He works hard and takes his work seriously. He's a little rough in his manner. While he's true to Captain Kirk and other crew members on the ship, he's very suspicious of strangers. He is straight-forward with others—one of his most often repeated lines is when Captain Kirk tells him to fix something in a certain amount of time because the life of the crew or some planet depends on it— Scotty comes back with, "You'll have to give me more time, Captain."

McCartney 2003

QUALITIES:

GREAT COMPANION

PLACES IMPORTANCE ON INTEGRITY

FEISTY IN A PLAYFUL WAY

BUSY WITH ACTIVITIES HE ENJOYS

FINE FOR NOVICE WOMEN

Behavior with children:

Exercise required:

Activity level:

Ease of training:

Sociability with strangers:

Affection level:

Playfulness:

Protectiveness:

Watchdog ability:

PHYSICAL CHARACTERISTICS: West Highland White Terrier men are dapper-looking guys with a friendly smile. They have a sparkle in their eyes. These men prefer a clean-cut and tidy look; however, some get complacent and can look a bit shaggy. Keeping up with them can be a challenge because one minute you see them and the next you don't.

ABILITIES & INTERESTS: Westie men are the friendliest and most outgoing of all the Terrier breeds of men. They will shine in any activity or career where they can work with others. They are curious, intelligent, and like to dig. They can uncover things others may not be able to find. People trust them and will reveal intimate details about their lives to these men. As friendly as these men are, they are still Terriers, and as such have a sixth sense for reading people. They can tell early on if someone is to be trusted or not. If not, they will not hesitate to let other people know about this person. Westies can sometimes take on a foe bigger than themselves, because Westies are tougher than they appear to be. Most Westie men today, however, spend less time tackling the injustices of the world and instead prefer to be companions to others. They are mostly motivated to spend time with others, playing and having fun. They have more energy than most people, and when others have stopped, they'll still be going, wondering what's wrong with everyone else. Westies enjoy exercise and will choose some activity that they can do with friends, whether it be jogging, tennis, golf, or such.

TRAINING: Training a Westie man is relatively easy, just be prepared for him to do things in his time. He will respond sooner rather than later, but, depending on how he is asked, it can take him longer than you are willing to wait. He can be a bit independent and stubborn at times. Praise works well as do rewards, especially rewards involving affection. Ignoring unwanted behavior and praising desired behavior will help. Turning work into play or involving others will encourage him to participate in activities that require his assistance. Stay away from games such as tug-of-war or one-upmanship, because he will be tenacious in his desire to win.

SOCIAL SKILLS: Westie men love people, no matter if they've known them for years or they've just met. People are drawn to these men's charismatic, charming personalities. They tend to have lots of friends so they don't have to be alone. At work, and during their time off, they'll find someone to be with. They like to stay busy, so they usually choose friends who can keep up with them. They can be good with older children, but infants are usually not their priority or of much interest to them. Changing diapers is a task they will try hard to avoid. These men can be extremely affectionate and loving as children grow older. In a relationship, Westie men are very affectionate and devoted. They will want to spend as much time as possible with their partners and also have time for their friends. These men can be very demanding in a relationship, wanting time and attention.

TYPE OF WOMAN: The best woman for a West Highland White Terrier man will enjoy spending a lot of time with this man. She'll appreciate his ability to go, go, go, and she'll be pleased by his extremely social nature. She'll not need him to assist much if they have young children. She'll trust his ability to understand people.

TYPICAL WEST HIGHLAND WHITE TERRIER MAN: David's story, as told by a friend, Jenny:

Something needed to change, but I wasn't sure what. I felt like something was missing. That I was here for a purpose that somebody forgot to tell me. I read self-help books, listened to the "experts" on radio and TV, I even attended workshops that I thought would help. I always learned something, but this other feeling still nagged at me.

Watching a beautiful sunset at the park, I heard this man standing next to me singing a song. The song was a song everyone knows, but the way he sang it gave it meaning that I'd never noticed before. After he had finished, I commented on my interpretation of the song. He smiled "You're very perceptive. I heard Wayne Dyer speak about this song, and ever since I find my self singing it throughout the day."

"I'm familiar with Wayne Dyer. I think I've read or listened to all the self-help gurus out there. And I'm still searching."

"For what?" asked David.

"For my purpose, why I'm here."

"Oh, that. I used to look for mine also. Then one day it dawned on me that I wasn't looking anymore. I realized I was living it. I'm not sure how I even got on it. It just happened. Obviously, it wasn't a big Aha! moment or I would have remembered it."

That seemed rather odd to me. Something must have led up to it. But he assured me it hadn't. We started meeting at the park and going for walks. David truly seemed to live in the moment and embrace life. He kept busy with activities and people he enjoyed. He had a happy-go-lucky manner that I admired. At the same time, he was well grounded. He didn't have his head too far in the clouds. I loved his cleverness with words. Sometimes, during our walks, he would tell me stories he made up. As a writer of technical articles for a major company, he enjoyed fiction as an outlet for his creativity.

I looked forward to our walks. David was the best friend I'd ever had —just being with him made me happy. Months went by, then a year; and then, one day, as we sang our song, the one David was singing when we first met, I felt so full of joy and happiness that I wasn't thinking about my purpose anymore. In fact, I hadn't thought about it for a long time—I was living it. And so I smiled as we sang those simple words that summed up life: "Row, row, row your boat, gently down the stream—merrily, merrily, merrily, merrily! Life is but a dream!"

FAMOUS WEST HIGHLAND WHITE TERRIER MAN: Adam Sandler as Robbie Hart in *The Wedding Singer*

Robbie's driven by his need for loving companionship. When his girlfriend leaves him at the altar, he's devastated. His friendship with Julia picks him back up. As a determined Terrier can, he helps Julia find and negotiate the best deals for her wedding needs. With integrity, he stands up to his girlfriend and refuses to take her back when he knows she's not right for him.

10

THE TOY GROUP

THE TOY GROUP of men have a strong desire to be pampered. They are also very affectionate but can still snap if they don't get their way. As long as they get enough love, they will try hard to please.

CHIHUAHUA: Although they're in a small package, these endearing guys can put on a tough guy act. They'll let you know where there is danger, even if they are unable to do much about it.

MALTESE: These smart guys are easy to spoil because they're too cute and sweet. They love attention . . . center stage is their home.

PEKINGESE: Sassy but sweet, these sensitive guys love to lie around and be waited on. They can be temperamental and, if you let them get away with it, become little tyrants.

PUG: They may seem a little odd, but these loveable guys will amuse you, even if that is not their intent. They have the sweetest hearts despite their gruff appearance.

SHIH TZU: These guys know what they want—attention and lots of petting. Of course they're so sweet and affectionate, it's easy to give it to them.

QUALITIES:

INTELLIGENT AND CREATIVE

NEEDS COMPANIONSHIP

BUSY GO-GETTER

VERY SENSITIVE

FINE FOR NOVICE WOMEN

Behavior with children:

Exercise required:

Activity level:

Ease of training:

Sociability with strangers:

Affection level:

Playfulness:

Protectiveness:

Watchdog ability:

PHYSICAL CHARACTERISTICS: Chihuahua men tend to be rather frail-looking. Many of these men will put up a tough front, while others will be shaking in their shoes at the smallest threat. They have big eyes and a pleading look that draws many women in. Always on the go, you may get one glimpse of a Chihuahua man before he's gone again.

ABILITIES & INTERESTS: A Chihuahua man's primary drive is to be a companion to one woman and for them to adore each other. Without someone to adore him and bond with, he may appear lost. These men are bright and are such busy go-getters that they can accomplish a great deal. If they have a loving woman by their side, nothing can stop them. If not, they may struggle to make something of themselves. Because their partners are so important to them, and they are so sensitive, if they are belittled by those partners they can be pathetic, sad men. They enjoy playing games that involve the mind such as chess, and they definitely prefer one-on-one games as opposed to group games. Chihuahua men can put up a protective front. Even though they may not be able to stop a real threat, they'll let everyone know when something's amiss. Exercise doesn't interest the Chihuahua man, and he's so busy it's almost impossible for him to get overweight.

TRAINING: Most Chihuahua men are fairly easy to train. They truly want to please the person they bond with, but at the same time, they can be head-strong. Consistency is very important, and the best way to appeal to a Chihuahua man is through lots of praise and big rewards. The biggest challenge with a Chihuahua man is his tendency to nip when things don't go his way. Most of the time it's annoying more than anything. Still, it is behavior that needs to be redirected. Completely ignoring him can often affect him more than anything else. Harsh words on top of his will only escalate because he interprets them as an affront to his masculinity. As long as he is adored and loved, he will return it back ten times, and he will try his best to please.

SOCIAL SKILLS: With strangers Chihuahua men tend to be shy, nervous, uninterested, or all three. Even after he knows someone, he may continue to be wary and perhaps nervous around them. Some Chihuahua men will have other male friends, but oftentimes not, and only occasionally will they form a close bond with a man. If a Chihuahua man is single, he is more likely to have a close friend, but even then, he usually prefers the company of a woman. Chihuahua men are not that great with children. They can tolerate them and sometimes will even deeply love their own. But they can nip if they feel infringed upon, and they especially dislike competing for their partner's attention. In a relationship, if a woman wants a man who will completely bond with her, who will want to spend all his time with her and will be happy to forsake all others, then she could find a Chihuahua man to be the perfect mate. These men can easily become jealous. And a jealous Chihuahua will sometimes take on more than he can handle and can even get himself into trouble. As long as a Chihuahua man feels confident in his relationship, he will make a superb, loving companion. The more he is adored, the more he will adore you back.

TYPE OF WOMAN: The woman most suited for a Chihuahua man will want a constant companion who will worship her and want to be loved in return. She'll understand his protective nature and his jealous streak. Whether or not a Chihuahua man wants to have friends or get together with other people will not matter to her. She will not need to have children, or she will be able to balance her love for him and the children in such a way that he does not feel threatened. Games they can play together will keep them connected in a fun way. She'll need to appreciate his constant high-energy, active lifestyle.

TYPICAL CHIHUAHUA MAN: Andy's story, as told by his wife, Ann:

I've always loved and adored my husband. Finding out that he's a Chihuahua fits perfectly and makes total sense why I cherish him like I do. You see, I raise Chihuahuas, and they are my precious babies. Andy is just like my Chihuahuas—he's playful, busy, loves being pampered, is protective in spirit (not in reality), intelligent, and creative.

My husband and I live a life of leisure due to a large inheritance. So we mostly play with our dogs and travel. I have a tendency to be somewhat bossy, or at least that's what other people have said. Anyway, on one of our trips in the motor home, Andy was driving and I was giving what I thought was good advice. "Andy, there's a good parking place there up ahead, on the right. No, not there . . . over there . . . so we'll be closer to the door. Then you can go inside and get the supplies we need. Now remember, just get what we need. Don't go buying anything else, and don't spend hours looking at magazines."

Andy sighed and said, "You treat me like I'm five years old."

Well, he was right. I don't mean to, it's just I have a strong instinct to mother. Now that I know he's a Chihuahua, it makes even more sense why I treat him the way I do. It's not that I think he's incapable of doing things. It's just that I'm used to telling the dogs what to do, and he seems like one of them. That may sound bad, but most people would love to be my dogs and receive as much love and affection as they do. A friend said, "When I come back after dying, I'm going to reincarnate as one of your dogs."

The other day, Andy said, "I need to pull over so I can poop."

"Okay" I said. "Go ahead."

Then he says, "I need to poop and pee, pee and poop. Yes, I have to poop, right now. A big poop and a long pee."

Once we stopped I looked at him and said, "And you wonder why I talk to you like you're five years old."

At first he looked hurt, then angry, and then he broke into a huge grin and laughed. Life is such a delight being married to a Chihuahua man. For me, it's heaven.

FAMOUS CHIHUAHUA MAN: Woody Allen as Val in *Hollywood Ending*

Val appears high strung, nervous, eccentric, needy, and moody, but despite all that, his ex-wife still wants him back, which goes to prove there's someone for everyone. Not to say he doesn't have wonderful qualities in the movie, because he does. He's intelligent, creative, sensitive, and a busy go-getter. At the beginning of the movie, we find out that after his wife left him, he had a hard time finding work because his creativity and ability to work with others deteriorated. Having her back in his life, believing in him, puts him back on track.

QUALITIES:

ACTIVE GO-GETTER

LOVING COMPANION

CONNOISSEUR OF FINE THINGS

PLAYFUL AND AFFECTIONATE

FINE FOR NOVICE WOMEN

Behavior with children:	🦴🦴
Exercise required:	🦴
Activity level:	🦴🦴🦴
Ease of training:	🦴🦴
Sociability with strangers:	🦴🦴
Affection level:	🦴🦴
Playfulness:	🦴🦴🦴
Protectiveness:	🦴
Watchdog ability:	🦴🦴🦴

PHYSICAL CHARACTERISTICS: Maltese men are very attractive. They are handsome in a feminine way. They hold their heads high and carry themselves with dignity. Appearances are very important to these guys, and they can spend almost as much time getting ready as some women. Their taste in clothes is exquisite, and they love to dress up.

ABILITIES & INTERESTS: Maltese men enjoy being taken care of, pampered, and adored. A life of leisure is the life for them. If absolutely necessary they can work, because they are quite clever and have an immense amount of energy, but their preference is to not work. They may also work due to their love of fine things and their excellent taste in whatever interests them, whether it be fine wine, antiques, cars, or such. These men have a wild side to them that most people won't know about until they truly get to know these guys. When they let their hair down, they know how to have fun, and these men can be extremely playful, even feisty. People can also be surprised by the boldness of Maltese men. If need be, these guys will take on something or someone twice their size or more. Unfortunately, they are not always as tough as they think they are and can run into trouble if they are not careful. Exercise is something the Maltese man isn't that interested in and usually does not need much of, in part because he is so active he can burn a lot of calories.

TRAINING: A Maltese man is fairly easy to train. The most challenging part is that he is so cute and can be so feisty in an adorable way that you sometimes inadvertently encourage poor behavior. As long as you are consistent in ignoring inappropriate behavior and rewarding good behavior he'll be easy. He will respond well to praise and reward, especially if the reward is play and affection. He will occasionally be slow in his response to a request, but he'll get around to it eventually—maybe after a few reminders and a few heavy sighs. A Maltese man is very, very sensitive. Scolding him or being harsh will make him despondent and sad. Few women have the heart to abuse these men because they are just too cute and sweet.

SOCIAL SKILLS: Maltese men are picky about the people they associate with. They can be very polite when need be to strangers, but will watch a person carefully before warming up to him. They enjoy the company of friends who they can truly be intimate with. Oftentimes their friends are women, because women, more than men, appreciate their sensitive natures and their love of fine things. If they have to work, they can be team players as long as they like the people they work with. Children sometimes require more attention than Maltese men are willing to give, especially young children. Usually, Maltese men prefer older children that they can play with and be affectionate with. If play turns too rough, however, they may walk away. In a relationship, these men are amazingly affectionate, devoted, and loving. They want to be pampered and will return the love in kind.

TYPE OF WOMAN: The woman for a Maltese man will appreciate giving and receiving lots of affection. She'll understand his desire to be treated as special and his love of fine things. Whether or not he is good with young children will not matter to her. She'll either have the energy to keep up with him or she will let him stay busy and not expect him to sit still for long.

TYPICAL MALTESE MAN: Ron's story, as told by his wife, Lynn:

"Ron is a Maltese. Are you familiar with the Maltese breed?" When Jeannette asked us that, we both started laughing. It took us a while to catch our breath. First of all, Ron's a big guy, and most people would not consider him a

Maltese based on size. However, anyone who knows Ron gets it. Jeannette looked concerned, so we reassured her, "That's perfect! We own a Maltese named Caesar, and Ron and Caesar are like twins. Both love being pampered and they are like the Energizer Bunny—they keep going and going . . ."

Ron and I own an Italian restaurant. It's homey, but we also offer a good selection of fine wines and specialty foods that we import direct from Italy. According to Ron, excellent service and delicious food make us the local favorite. The restaurant is his love. We start the day at the restaurant at 9:00 AM sharp and rarely leave before midnight, six days a week. Caesar goes with us and stays in the back office. We rarely take time off. For ten years we've only taken one week off each year—our annual trip to Italy.

Six months ago, I was hanging Christmas decorations at the restaurant when I lost my balance and fell off the ladder. Ron rushed to my side.

"Lynn, honey, are you okay? Did you hurt yourself?"

"Ron, I think I broke my leg."

Sure enough, I had. Ron rushed me to the emergency room, demanded immediate attention (in a nice way), and held my hand the whole time. When we got home, the medication kicked in and I slept. When I woke up, Ron was on one side of me, and Caesar was on the other. "Hi, guys," I said groggily. They both sat up, concern in their eyes. Ron said, "How do you feel, Lynn? Can I get you anything? Water? Food? Pillows?"

I smiled, "I'm okay, thanks. How long have I been here?"

"Four hours."

"And you've been here the whole time, Ron?"

"Of course. Caesar and I wouldn't leave you in your time of need."

"What about the restaurant?" I asked.

"Rick's in charge. I told him I'll be back in a week or two."

I was stunned. "Ron, you can't leave the restaurant that long. You'll go crazy here."

"It's my decision, Lynn. Right now my place is with you. Caesar and I talked about it, and we agree. You are always there for me, taking care of me. It's my turn to give to you. Besides, we can catch up on movies." He leaned over and kissed me and I giggled. Lying in bed, tucked between my two Maltese, Ron and Caesar, I felt no pain.

FAMOUS MALTESE MAN: Owen Wilson as Hansel in *Zoolander*

Hansel is the model who won "Male Model of the Year" four years in a row. He's surrounded by a group of eclectic people who travel with him. His furnishings are a cornucopia of exquisite, exotic pieces. He's a sweet, gentle guy who's always stylishly dressed. When it comes to dueling, he chooses runways and break-dancing as his weapons rather than pistols.

©McCartney/2003

QUALITIES:

ENJOYS BEING PAMPERED AND PAMPERING OTHERS

APPRECIATES FINE THINGS

PREFERS A LIFE OF LEISURE

VERBALLY PROTECTIVE

FINE FOR NOVICE WOMEN

Behavior with children:

Exercise required:

Activity level:

Ease of training:

Sociability with strangers:

Affection level:

Playfulness:

Protectiveness:

Watchdog ability:

PHYSICAL CHARACTERISTICS: Pekingese men may not be the biggest guys around, but they are proud, often arrogant, and will carry themselves as such. For some reason, they are able to pull off this attitude without offending too many people. They are very particular about their appearance. Even when in a casual mode they are very neat. They look friendly, and yet people sometimes wonder if they truly are.

ABILITIES & INTERESTS: Pekingese men believe that they are here to be served. Being pampered and made much over is their favorite pastime. Usually they do best working for themselves, because few bosses understand how special these men are or how special they think they are. Although they may not be major go-getters, Pekingese men are very bright, and they can be successful in life if they find something they enjoy. The more others look up to them and treat them with respect in a work environment, the more they will enjoy their work. The Pekingese man is not just a lap-dog man. He'll let others know, in advance, of approaching danger. He's courageous and can put up a fierce front when pushed too hard. These men are also calm and enjoy taking life easy. They prefer not to exercise because it's too much work. But they need it.

TRAINING: A Pekingese man is fairly challenging to train because he is intelligent and he thinks he should be served by others. At the same time, if it suits him, a Pekingese can be cooperative and helpful. As long as he is given lots of praise, rewards, and treated like he's special, he'll try to please. The key to a Pekingese man is allowing him to occasionally dig his heels in and say "No" without berating him. He can be moody, and his disobedience is more a reflection of his desires and mood than of how much he loves or respects you. He can snap if pushed too hard and, while he won't do much damage, it can still hurt. You need to balance treating him like he is special and at the same time not allowing him to dominate you in an aggressive manner.

SOCIAL SKILLS: Pekingese men can be friendly if they want to be, but usually they don't care to be. They don't care what strangers think of them and, unless they have something to gain they see little need to go out of their way to meet and be friendly to new people. If they decide to approach someone, they can be extremely charming. These men do not need a wide circle of friends. They may or may not have a few friends they get together with. They can be good with children if they really want them and, usually, they are most helpful when the children are older. As long as children don't get too rowdy, a Pekingese will enjoy playing with them. In a relationship, Pekingese men can be very loyal and devoted when they want to be. They love pampering and adoring others as well as being on the receiving end.

TYPE OF WOMAN: The woman most suited for a Pekingese man will recognize and honor his need to be treated like royalty. She will be independent, smart, and playful. She can stand her ground, and yet let him say "No" and do what he needs to do at times. The couple's cuddling and pampering one another is something she will appreciate.

TYPICAL PEKINGESE MAN: Charles' story, as told by his wife, Meagan:

Two reasons I married Charles: First, he had ambition and was successful. I admired that. Growing up just above poverty made me long for more. I wanted financial security. I wouldn't say I was shallow, just realistic. He treated me like a queen. Anything I wanted he would get for me—a car, a maid, jewelry. I also wanted love, which takes me to the second reason I married

Charles. We truly loved one another. What more could a girl ask for?

Life was good for 20 years. Charles continued to pamper me with affection and presents. One morning, when our children were gone, I realized I was bored. I decided to return to school. I had always wanted to study architecture and be an architect. Charles consented, and I was excited. Soon my life was full with exams and projects. My attention shifted from Charles to school. It was subtle at first, but then it continued to grow. I felt as if my life had meaning and purpose, and I was filled with a passion I didn't know I possessed. That's when the trouble started.

Charles pampered me, but I realized in part it was because I pampered him. As I became more involved in my studies, he became more resentful. As my passion for my work grew, he became more suspicious of me. What brought out this fiery side that he had never seen? He assumed the worst and thought I was having an affair. For the first time in our relationship, he became a tyrant. He was demanding, wanting to know where I was going, and when I would be back. I wondered why he would think I was having an affair unless he was. I became spiteful and mean. How dare he accuse me of having an affair, and how dare he resent my quest for a better life! One that gave me purpose! I came really close to walking out on the relationship. And, as embarrassing as it may sound, the only thing keeping me in was the financial situation.

At dinner one night Charles said, "Meagan, we can't go on like this. Something has to change."

"Yes, Charles I agree. How about counseling?"

"I don't like the idea of someone else knowing our business." And that was the end of the conversation. But it made me think. Perhaps I could go to a counselor at school. I wouldn't have to tell him. So I did. I was skeptical about seeing a therapist, but, fortunately, the man I saw was excellent. He used a method called Psych-K to uncover my subconscious beliefs. What I came to realize was how I had let Charles treat me with disrespect and talk down to me for years, all because he gave me things. Over the years, his treatment of me had worsened. Regardless of the consequences, it was time for me to stand up for myself.

Charles was thrown into chaos. He didn't know how to respond to the boundaries I set. In the past when he insulted me, I would take it. Now, in a calm voice, I would say, "Charles, I don't like how you're talking to me."

Eventually, it became too much. He found a younger woman who was impressed by the presents. She thought he was the most wonderful man she had ever met.

Me, I'm the happiest I've ever been. I'm working for an architect on projects I enjoy. Most important, I like myself and have a confidence I never knew existed. This may not be the "fairy-tale ending" I grew up with . . . but maybe it's time to rewrite those stories.

FAMOUS PEKINGESE MAN: Ryan Phillippe as Sebastian Valmont in *Cruel Intentions*

Although Sebastian at first appears cold-hearted, self-centered, and spoiled, he changes after meeting Annette. He still appreciates the "good life" and being pampered, like all Pekingese, but Annette's well-being and happiness become equally important to him. He goes out of his way and against his past behavior to do what's best for her. This is evident in the scene where she wants to have sex and he refuses her. In the end, he goes so far as to make the ultimate sacrifice for her.

QUALITIES:

PLAYFUL AND SWEET

CLEVER AND CREATIVE

ENJOYS TAKING IT EASY

LOYAL AND DEVOTED

FINE FOR NOVICE WOMEN

Behavior with children:

Exercise required:

Activity level:

Ease of training:

Sociability with strangers:

Affection level:

Playfulness:

Protectiveness:

Watchdog ability:

PHYSICAL CHARACTERISTICS: These men are less intimidating-looking than a Mastiff, although there is a similarity between them. They can appear tough, but in a soft way that draws people to them more than repelling them. The Pug man usually has a thoughtful look on his face, and when he's not concentrating on something else, he has an intriguing smile. Pug men are very casual in their dress, and people may at times wonder if they own an iron.

ABILITIES & INTERESTS: Pug men first and foremost just want to enjoy life and take it easy. They like to play—not too roughly, though. They are intelligent and enjoy board or card games. Given a choice, they would love being men of leisure. Unfortunately, most of them have to do something to get by, and when they put their minds to it they are quite capable. They may not work as hard as everyone around them, but they can be successful in business if something ignites their passion. They are observant of what goes on around them and can alert people to danger long before others realize what is happening. They may not do more than alerting people, but that ability can be a lifesaver. Exercise is a good idea for these men, although they do not need much. A little romp usually suits them fine. Hot weather does not work for them. Outdoor exercise works only when it is temperate or cool.

TRAINING: A Pug man can be easy to train as long as you work with him and appreciate his desire to take his time. Don't expect him to respond immediately when he is asked to do something. If it suits him, and he is asked nicely, he'll do what he can. Occasionally he can be stubborn, but most of the time he just likes to do things in his own way. He's not trying to be difficult. The more you get frustrated by a Pug man and become forceful, the worse he will respond. Too much criticism and he can become a complete wimp. Lots of praise, playfulness, and rewards will work wonders.

SOCIAL SKILLS: Pug men can be friendly and right away can tell if they like a person or not. Friends that like to play games such as chess or engage in interesting conversation are important to a Pug man. Pugs can also be perfectly content alone reading a book, watching television, or some other activity that requires little effort. With children, these men are excellent. Children love them and know that Pug men are safe playmates. Pug men put emphasis on family and will do the best they can to have happy families. In relationships, these men are very loyal and affectionate. They don't require a lot of attention, but they appreciate it, and they respond so much better when they receive tender loving care.

TYPE OF WOMAN: The best woman for a Pug man will appreciate him regardless of how much he does. She'll understand if he is not a real go-getter. She'll enjoy his playfulness and intelligence, and she'll want to join him in activities that he enjoys (hopefully she enjoys them too). Although he will not require a lot from her, she will enjoy providing praise and affection every day.

TYPICAL PUG MAN: Jason's story, as told by his wife, Linda:

Jason and I knew each other and were friends for five years before we got married. How we finally got married is a bizarre story. We first met at a friend's birthday party. The next time we saw each other was a month later at another friend's housewarming party. Realizing we had a lot of the same friends, we started seeing each other at more events. We got along. Jason made me laugh with his cute antics, although sometimes he wasn't trying to be funny. He just was.

Jason's motto is "Follow the path of least resistance." Over the years, I witnessed this lifestyle approach in many forms. When he lost his job, he didn't rush out to find another one. He didn't even worry about what he would do next. He just waited until something appropriate came his way, and eventually it did. Occasionally he would show up at events with different women. Many times other friends set them up. He seemed to enjoy their company, but they didn't last long.

Then, on St Patrick's Day at a local bar, a group of us got together to celebrate. At some point in the evening, Jason and I were alone while I think everyone else was on the dance floor or playing pool. All of a sudden, I had this image of what it would be like to be married to Jason. He was kind, sensitive, and fun. I thought about all the jerks I'd dated and knew Jason was different. I don't know if it was the green beers or what, but right there I said, "Jason, let's get married."

"Okay," he said, "When do you want to get married?"

I figured he wasn't taking me seriously, probably too many beers on both sides, but I said, "How about next week?"

"Sounds good to me." That night he never said another word about it.

The next afternoon, he called me up and said, "I talked to the priest down the street and he couldn't marry us for another month. However, the Justice of the Peace can fit us in Thursday."

I was shocked. "Jason, I didn't think you took me seriously!"

"Well yeah, I thought you were. Did you change your mind?"

"No, let's go ahead and do it Thursday. We can always do the church thing later if we want."

Within a few days we were married, much to the amazement of our friends.

Well, five years and two children later, we're still happily married. I've made a lot of decisions in my life, but by far the best decision I ever made was asking Jason to marry me.

FAMOUS PUG MAN: George on *Seinfeld*

George has various jobs at times, and he can be successful, but what he prefers most is a life of leisure, hanging out with friends and taking life a little slower than those around him. Occasionally he'll come across as tough, but few people are really intimidated by him. Like the time he went to an Anger-aholics meeting. In the midst of his temper tantrum, he appeared funny and cute. To his close friends, he's very loyal. George can also be cynical and snide in a playful way.

McCARTNEY/2008

QUALITIES:

PATIENT

GOOD TASTE IN FINE THINGS

SENSITIVE AND CARING

A GREAT LOVING COMPANION

FINE FOR NOVICE WOMEN

Behavior with children: 🦴 🦴

Exercise required: 🦴

Activity level: 🦴 🦴

Ease of training: 🦴 🦴

Sociability with strangers: 🦴 🦴

Affection level: 🦴 🦴 🦴

Playfulness: 🦴 🦴 🦴

Protectiveness: 🦴 🦴

Watchdog ability: 🦴 🦴

PHYSICAL CHARACTERISTICS: Appearances are important to this well-groomed man. He likes every hair in its place. He pays particular attention to dress, and even in sweats he is stylish. Shih Tzu men generally have silky smooth hair, and women love to run their fingers through it, even if the men have little hair left. They're cheerful men and often carry a smile to light your day. Some Shih Tzu men appear arrogant because they carry their heads high and have a slightly flippant air about them. Don't be fooled, though. They're sweethearts and will usually make time for you.

ABILITIES & INTERESTS: Shih Tzu men are companionable by nature. Whatever profession they choose, it will involve people. Some may work in sales, others in health care, as long as they have interaction with others. A Shih Tzu man's favorite pastime is being pampered, petted, and loved. At work and at home, he'll look for an environment that is conducive to being appreciated. Beauty draws Shih Tzu men for miles. Art museums and galleries are personal favorite hangout spots of theirs. They have great taste in clothes and furnishings, and women often love to take them shopping because they'll trust a Shih Tzu man's good taste and honesty. Shih Tzu men are very playful and fun to be around. They enjoy playing games like Pictionary, Monopoly, Charades and other games that require human interaction. Outdoor games and sports are less interesting to them than indoor games—they're not big on exercise. Shih Tzu men need to exercise even though they would prefer not to.

TRAINING: Even if you pamper a Shih Tzu man, chances are you won't spoil him. He's just too good-natured. And while he may not respond to your requests as soon as you would like, he'll eventually do what you ask. The most effective method of training involves lots of praise, play, and reward. Rewards for a Shih Tzu are different from rewards for many other breeds. You may have to study him and try different incentives to see what works best. The only caution with a Shih Tzu is not to jerk him around. He may lack the fierceness of a Doberman when pushed too far, but he could still snap. He gets especially irritable when he is too hot.

SOCIAL SKILLS: Since Shih Tzu men are companions by nature, they are friendly and easygoing with almost everyone. With strangers, they are polite but not pushy. They usually let you come to them. They are easy to talk to and be around. They can be assertive and feisty although they may hide it initially. The more you get to know them, the more their feistiness comes through. When it comes to children, a Shih Tzu man can be good with older children. Some are less at ease with toddlers. If you want children, watch him around babies and see how he responds. He may be better with his own children, but be prepared for him to hand a screaming baby back to you. He's so loving and affectionate that he usually makes a great father. However, make sure that you give him enough attention. They are extremely loyal and devoted to those they love. If you like being cuddled and you want a man who enjoys spending time together, you'll be delighted with a Shih Tzu man.

TYPE OF WOMAN: The best woman for a spunky Shih Tzu man will want to love, pamper, and spend long hours with her man. She'll appreciate his strong feminine side. Although he may not want to play many outdoor sports, the woman for a Shih Tzu man will want to play other kinds of games with him. She'll be prepared for his wanting to spend time with friends, possibly other women friends. It will help if she's confident enough in herself to know he can be trusted.

TYPICAL SHIH TZU MAN: Ray's story, as told by himself:

Presently I'm a doctor, but I prefer to be known as a health and wellness facilitator. I help facilitate people through their healing process and give them the strategies to self-heal. There is no greater satisfaction for me than to see people grow and evolve into the types of persons they deserve to be.

Prior to being a doctor, I helped people feel and look their best by helping them learn how to coordinate fashion. I have a good fashion sense, and I worked as a manager for Nordstrom in the men's clothing department. At Nordstrom, you had to always have a smile on your face regardless of how difficult the situation was, and there were times when there were some pretty challenging customers. However, my entire life I've been told I have the patience of a saint. Due to my patient nature, I developed a large customer following that consisted of many clients whom most of the staff would run away from screaming. Yet I found that if I treated people with kindness and respect they would eventually open up and reciprocate, regardless of their initial less-than-pleasant dispositions.

As an example of this, I remember there was one couple in particular who would come in every two months or so to check out what was new. The wife was very sweet, pleasant, and understanding. The husband was gruff, rude, and ill-tempered. I remember my very first dealing with Mr. and Mrs. Smith. They wanted a particular style suit in a particular color. He tried on suit after suit. Each one he would hem and haw about. And then, after consulting his wife, he would make the tailor pin up the suit in various areas to make it fit better. This process often took as much as 15 minutes per suit. After trying on about 20 suits, Mr. Smith still had not decided on one he liked. There was one he liked in a size that wasn't even close to his. So I called around to about 35 of our other stores before I found the suit in the proper size for Mr. Smith. Fortunately, this garment suited Mr. Smith's taste and the fit was to his liking. However, before he committed to buying the suit, he had to outfit it with "just the right" shirt and tie. At our particular Nordstrom store, we usually had about 2,000 different styles of ties and 60 different shirt styles. After several hours of trying various combinations, Mr. Smith didn't find one to his liking. So now he decided not to get the suit.

After all this investment of time, your average person would probably give up. However, I didn't want to give up. I said to myself, I am going to sell this man a suit if it's the last thing I do. The Smiths went home that day without purchasing anything.

Several weeks later, a new shipment of suits came in. There were a few I thought Mr. Smith might like. I phoned the Smiths and invited them to come take a look at them. After consulting his wife, Mr. Smith decided on a navy herringbone suit with very subtle pinstripes. We headed over to the shirt and tie area and, after several hours, came up with a combination that was satisfactory to the Smiths.

I worked with them for about a year before I was transferred to another Nordstrom store in another state. I'd been at my newest Nordstrom location for about nine months when I was bestowed one of the highest honors given to Nordstrom staff, the Customer Service All-Star award. This award is usually given to people who give consistently great customer service or to someone who goes above and beyond the call of duty. At one of our manager's meetings the general manager started to read a letter from a customer. It was written by a man who was describing how his wife had died suddenly several months ago from cancer. He went on to say how devastated he had been, and that it had been difficult for him to get on with his normal daily routine. During his several months of feeling extremely low, he finally remembered he had promised his wife something. She had asked him to write a letter to commend the suit salesman who had shown them such care and kindness over the last year. The husband said he needed to pick himself up, so he wrote that it was among the highlights of his wife's last year to go into Nordstrom and be so wholeheartedly taken care of by a salesperson who really had a genuine interest in taking care of her and her husband and meeting their needs. He said that she hoped there would be more people like that salesman around who would be able to take care of her husband once she was no longer around. The man went on to say that he was not fond of dealing with salespeople, but that he also was moved by the consideration and actions of this young man and that he should be recognized for his tremendous service. My general manager ended the letter by saying, "It was signed by Mr. Smith."

I was extremely touched by this letter, as was everyone around me. It was at this moment that the general manager called me up in front of our group. Only then did I realize that this was the same couple I had worked with at the previous Nordstrom. I stood there with such joy that I was able to touch this couple with my actions, but I also reflected back on those times when I had asked myself whether I should continue working with these people because it took so much time, energy and effort. That was when the general manager presented me with the prestigious Customer Service All-Star award. I am so thankful I didn't give up.

Famous Shih Tzu Man: Niles on *Frasier*

Niles is a sweet but feisty Shih Tzu who puts on a good "I'm better than you" act. He never has to be alone since he spends time with his father and brother and is involved with many groups. Niles has a stubborn streak but can be coaxed into things by Daphne's sweet talk. Beautiful décor, nice clothes, and fine wines are all important to Niles.

11

THE NON-SPORTING GROUP

L IKE DOG BREEDS, the Non-Sporting Group of men have nothing in common with each other. They also have nothing in common with the other breeds, so they are placed in a group by themselves.

BULLDOG: These lumbering guys appear rough, but they're usually big pushovers. They're a little slow to get things done because they prefer to lie around.

CHOW CHOW: These very protective guys may not appear as fierce as they can be. They can snap if provoked, and it doesn't take much to provoke them.

DALMATIAN: Many women think they want one of these attractive guys, but their exuberance and independence can make them a challenge for most women.

POODLE: These highly intelligent, creative guys are great showmen. Give them an audience and they can impress anyone.

©MCARTNEY
2003

QUALITIES:

FAMILY-ORIENTED

SENSITIVE DESPITE A TOUGH APPEARANCE

ABILITY TO LIE AROUND AND JUST BE

DESIRE TO PLEASE, EVEN IF HE DOESN'T ALWAYS PERFORM

FINE FOR NOVICE WOMEN

Behavior with children:

Exercise required:

Activity level:

Ease of training:

Sociability with strangers:

Affection level:

Playfulness:

Protectiveness:

Watchdog ability:

PHYSICAL CHARACTERISTICS: Bulldog men are tough, gruff, intimidating-looking men, but people seem drawn to them, perhaps because they exude power. They may move with a swagger but a little slower than those around them. These men tend to like the casual look. Most of the time, they are fairly neat and well groomed, and usually sport a cut that is easy to maintain.

ABILITIES & INTERESTS: Bulldog men seem like tough guys, but they have very soft, tender personalities. Compared to similar-looking breeds, they are not very protective. They can be accomplished if need be, but they would prefer to work less and play more. A life of leisure suits them. Bulldog men enjoy being paid attention to and taken care of. If these men find an activity or career they enjoy, they are capable of working hard. Of course, they'll go at their own pace, and hurrying them may be fruitless. These men are very steadfast and will hold firm to what they believe in. Although they can be stubborn, Bulldog men are very low-key, and it takes a lot to rile them. They enjoy playtime but avoid tug-of-war because they almost always win. They need exercise even if it means dragging them to it. Extreme heat should be avoided when exercising. These men have a tendency to snore when they sleep, so beware.

TRAINING: Training a Bulldog man is possible because he likes to please and will try to please. The only challenge is his slightly stubborn nature and desire to do things in his own time. Fortunately, he is so laid-back and easygoing that his stubbornness may not show itself very often. Doing things when he wants, according to his timetable, may be a consistent pattern. Remember: "Patience is a virtue." If needed, repeat this as your "dogma". When called upon in a pinch, he can come through in a timely fashion because he does care and is a sweetheart of a guy. He can take rough treatment, but I strongly encourage a loving approach. He's just too sweet to abuse. He appreciates praise and often needs encouragement to do what is asked of him. He tends to be protective of his food, and at mealtime he may slap the hand that reaches for his food.

SOCIAL SKILLS: Bulldog men can be very polite to strangers, although their gruff look can keep some people at a distance for a while. At the same time, people are often drawn to them and want to meet them. These men may not need a lot of friends, but they do appreciate a few close friendships. With people they are close to, Bulldog men can be extremely loyal and devoted. They can be content by themselves, reading, watching television, working on the computer, or just taking it easy. Children usually adore these loving men, and the feeling is mutual. Bulldog men are gentle, and they can take rough horseplay from children. Kids will react with caution when a Bulldog man gets upset. But children also seem to recognize his loving nature, good heart, and know a Bulldog man would never hurt them. In a relationship, he can be loving, loyal, and gentle. He will appreciate attention but not be greedy for it. A Bulldog man tends to be an easy companion.

TYPE OF WOMAN: The best woman for a Bulldog man appreciates his strength and power along with his gentle spirit. She understands he will approach life at his own pace, and she may not be able to speed him up. If he becomes stubborn, she'll ignore him, be patient, and realize he may not change his mind no matter what. She'll appreciate his love of children and his comical nature.

TYPICAL BULLDOG MAN: Steve's story, as told by his wife, Julie:
    Our daughter Sophia was born at home. She was healthy and robust and

we were very excited to have a little girl in addition to our three-year-old son. I had some postpartum complications and needed a lot of assistance, even in getting out of bed to go to the bathroom, the first days after giving birth. So the responsibility of taking care of a bedridden wife, a jilted three-year-old son, not to mention a brand-new baby girl, was all on Steve's shoulders, just following constant attendance by my side throughout a 19-hour labor and delivery. Steve was very tired and moving through a fog for the first few days of almost no sleep and very busy days of caretaking.

It was Sophia's third night in our home, and she, of course, was waking frequently and needing many diaper changes due to her voracious nursing! Steve needed to do all diaper changes since I was not yet strong enough. I remember lying in bed watching Steve get up and gently pick up Sophia with a shower of little kisses to bring her to the changing table. Well, not only was it a wet and poopy diaper, it was a "blowout" and he needed to change her entire outfit (which is not an easy task with a squirmy, curled-up newborn). Amid all of this, Steve was cheerful and sweet, talking to Sophia and giving her lots of kisses and engaging in soft conversation. As he was choosing a new outfit for her, I heard him say, "Look, Sophia, your first pink sleeper! This is a big moment in a girl's life—this and prom."

I had a new appreciation for the depth of his gentleness, admiration, and love for his daughter. I could just visualize him on some future prom night, gazing upon his grown daughter and beaming with that same joy, pride, and love he showed at that moment looking upon her little newborn face. I continue to marvel at how his face softens and his eyes light up when he is watching her. She moves through all layers of his intellect and seriousness in the blink of an eye to reveal his true essence of kindness, sweetness, and love.

I love my Bulldog!

Famous Bulldog Man: Drew Carey on *Drew Carey*

Drew has a tough-guy swagger, but he is a sweet, pussycat kind of guy. He enjoys life and plays as much as possible. He's funny even when he's not trying to be, and his humor is a little odd. His friends love and adore him because he's an all-around great guy. Does he get much work done?

©McCartney/2003

QUALITIES:

PROTECTIVE
DESIRE TO TAKE LIFE SLOW AND EASY
STRONG-WILLED
EXTREMELY LOYAL AND DEPENDABLE

FOR EXPERIENCED WOMEN DUE TO: STUBBORNNESS AND AGGRESSIVENESS

Behavior with children:

Exercise required:

Activity level:

Ease of training:

Sociability with strangers:

Affection level:

Playfulness:

Protectiveness:

Watchdog ability:

PHYSICAL CHARACTERISTICS: Chow Chow men are teddy-bearish in their look, and they wear an expression of concern or sadness on their faces. These sturdy men are very solid and carry themselves with some dignity. Keeping this man groomed requires work, and sometimes more than he is willing to do. Therefore, he may look a bit unkempt. For some of these men, the extra work is worth it to appear handsome and striking.

ABILITIES & INTERESTS: The Chow men are very serious men with incredibly strong instincts for guarding and watching over things and people. Although they are very laid-back most of the time and may not appear to be paying attention, the minute something is amiss, they are on top of it. They will not hesitate to take action against any wrongdoer. They are usually good judges of character, but a Chow might go after someone unjustly because he is suspicious of him. More than one innocent person has felt the wrath of a Chow man. There are also many fine Chow men who think before they act and are slow to anger. Pay attention to and watch a Chow man to really understand his particular nature. Chow men rarely hunt, but they are capable of pursuing something or someone when they are so inclined. With their incredible amount of focus and determination they can get things done if they feel drawn to do them. Self-employment works best for these men, especially careers where they do not have to deal with others very often. Exercise is beneficial to these men, but watch out for the heat. When it's hot outside, they need a gym where they can jog or lift weights.

TRAINING: Training a Chow man is easy enough if approached carefully. He is independent and very stubborn. He also likes to take life slow and easy. The most effective approach is lots of praise and huge rewards. A Chow man is picky about the type of reward that works for him, but once you find it, keep using it. Ignore unwanted behavior and, most important, do not be physically or verbally harsh with a Chow man. He can anger easily, and it may appear as if he's not upset and then, when you're not expecting it, he can attack. If he ever responds in a violent way, get help immediately. A well-trained Chow is wonderful, so find a well-trained one or find a fresh one willing to learn and train him well, using lots of love.

SOCIAL SKILLS: A Chow man is very suspicious of strangers, rarely letting anyone near him or his loved ones. Most of the time he will keep to himself and only occasionally let in other people whom he knows and trusts. He has little need for friends. One or two are enough, and even these he may not spend much time with. The Chow man can be very good with older children. He doesn't have much to do with toddlers. He may be very loving of his own children but has little tolerance for other children. Because he can be intimidating, his children's friends may prefer to play at their own or other children's houses. In a relationship, he can be independent and extremely protective. He is not overly affectionate; however, he is very devoted and loyal. He will be steadfast in his relationship.

TYPE OF WOMAN: The Chow man requires a very special kind of woman. She must be independent and very self-confident with an easy and consistent temper. She must be prepared for and appreciate his extremely protective nature, along with his need to take life slow and easy. If they have children, his wife will watch him carefully to understand how he will behave around them.

TYPICAL CHOW CHOW MAN: Bob's story, as told by his wife, Betty:

How did I end up marrying Bob? I know people wonder even though they don't ask. It's a good question. How did I marry a man so different from myself? Two reasons: Craig and Larry, my ex-husbands. Genetics pro-vides the makeup of who we are, but our experiences determine what we do with that genetic makeup. At least that's what I believe. My experiences with my exes led me into Bob's arms.

Craig and Larry, like me, are social. They enjoy going to parties, the opera, concerts, get-togethers with friends. But aside from that, when we were away from others and by ourselves, we fought. Both of them had girl-friends on the side and lied to me. I couldn't trust them to do what they said they would do, even simple things like going to the grocery store on their way home. Both of them were so caught up in other activities they were rarely home. In retrospect, I can't blame them. I was as much at fault in my own way. But I realized I was picking men based on one quality and not paying attention to my other, more important needs. One of my most basic needs is loyalty. I want to know that I am loved and cherished above all other women.

After Larry and I divorced, I was more cautious. When Bob first asked me out, I was doubtful. He was handsome in a rugged way, but he seemed distant and hard-edged. Still, what the heck, I said, "Yes." It took awhile for him to grow on me. He wasn't socially outgoing, he could be harsh with people, and he didn't like to do much—other than his work as a jew-elry craftsman. We seemed so different and yet we understood and appre-ciated one another. I didn't think I would ever marry again, but when Bob proposed, I said I would. Then I spent every day before the wedding pray-ing and hoping I had made the right decision. On our wedding day, we were late getting to the church, the singer was hoarse, Bob and one of the groomsmen were mad at each other, and the ring bearer cried while walk-ing down the aisle. Were these "signs" that we shouldn't get married?

We were going up to the honeymoon suite at the hotel, when my best friend, Kate, stopped me and said she needed to talk. I thought it odd that she picked that moment to ask me about some trivial item, but after a long time, I finally managed to break away and go upstairs. Bob had already gone up. When I walked inside the room, there was a trail of red roses, like a red carpet leading from the door to the bed. On the bed was a beautiful, sexy red nightgown and next to it was Bob in a red satin robe with a red tie on. "Betty, I know we're different, and I may not be perfect, but I am a man of my word, and I promise you, I will always love and cherish you the way you deserve." He's kept his promise. So although other people wonder about us, I don't.

FAMOUS CHOW CHOW MAN: Jack Nicholson as Melvin Udall in *As Good As It Gets*

Unpredictable, harsh, opinionated, stubborn, aggressive—those are a few of the characteristics displayed by Melvin in the movie. How could anyone love a man like that? The answer is, not everyone could, but all it takes is one woman who sees the good in him; a woman who recognizes that under all that gruff exterior there is a compassionate man. When his gay neighbor, Simon, needs help, and when the waitress, Carol, who waits on him needs help, Melvin is there. One hint into his true nature is Simon's dog who loves Melvin despite some harsh treatment early in the movie.

QUALITIES:

TIRELESS IN HIS PURSUIT

EAGER TO PLEASE OTHERS

SELF-ABSORBED

INTELLIGENT, GOOD PROBLEM SOLVER

FOR EXPERIENCED WOMEN DUE TO: STUBBORNNESS (SOME) AND AGGRESSIVENESS

Behavior with children:

Exercise required:

Activity level:

Ease of training:

Sociability with strangers:

Affection level:

Playfulness:

Protectiveness:

Watchdog ability:

PHYSICAL CHARACTERISTICS: Dalmatian men have "star quality" and most people notice them from the moment they walk into a room. Generally they are extremely attractive, and they carry themselves well. Because they are so active, they are usually in great physical shape. They are particular about their appearance, and their dress reflects this.

ABILITIES & INTERESTS: Dalmatian men have many talents and usually succeed at whatever they put their attention to. They push themselves hard and at times appear tireless. Because they are so striking, they are often used as front men and are seen on television, movies, and in advertising. They can be very protective, and usually this protective nature comes out only when necessary; however, some Dalmatian men can be easily riled. Dalmatian men love activity, including physical activity. They may be team players in group sports, but they also enjoy running, lifting weights, and other physical activities done by themselves. They have such a high demand for physical activity that they can become irritable and difficult when they do not get enough. Be prepared when they decide to play, because their play can be very exuberant.

TRAINING: Training a Dalmatian man can be challenging, mainly because he's so wound-up, going in high gear, that he's not always aware of what is being asked of him. He does have a desire to please others, and he is intelligent, but he may misunderstand what others want. The most important thing to keep in mind when working with a Dalmatian man is that he gets enough exercise. Next, provide an input-free environment so there are no distractions when communicating with him. That way, he can focus. Lastly, be clear in your communication with him and reward him when he does what you want. If you forget to reward him, he'll try anything to get approval, and it may not be what you want.

SOCIAL SKILLS: Dalmatian men can be friendly with strangers, but usually someone has to come up to them. Sometimes people approach them because they are so handsome, and sometimes people stay away for the same reason. Depending on the person, the Dalmatian man may respond favorably or not. Dalmatian men are often put on a pedestal, and sometimes they find it hard to live up to. They like having a circle of friends for sports and playtime. As fathers, Dalmatians are excellent because they truly love children. This is one of the places where their protective nature really kicks in. In a relationship, they can be extremely affectionate, sometimes more affectionate than a woman may be prepared for.

TYPE OF WOMAN: The woman for a Dalmatian will know that this beautiful package is much more challenging than it appears to be. She must appreciate his high energy. She'll respect him, let him know how special he is, and, at the same time, not put him on such a high pedestal that he cannot live up to her expectations. She'll recognize his need to be protective. And she will be clear in her communication and use rewards to let him know what she needs.

TYPICAL DALMATIAN MAN: Mitch's story, as told by his wife, Lily:

Women tell me all the time, "You're so lucky. You have the best husband. He's so handsome. He's so giving. So nice. So accomplished. I'd love to be in your shoes." And I think—if they only knew. They don't have a clue what it's like being married to him.

Mitch would give me the world if he thought I wanted it. The key here is "if he thought." He doesn't always stop to ask me what I want. He's so in his own world he doesn't always think about me and that we are different. It may sound like I'm being ungrateful. I'm not. I've learned over the years, however, to be crystal clear in my communication with Mitch. Otherwise, there's no end to his creative imaginings of what I want. A perfect example is my birthday last May.

I told Mitch I wanted a quiet birthday with just our family. What I didn't say, but should have said, was I don't want to have to do much either. The morning of my birthday, Mitch said, "I have a surprise for you. Just come with me." He took our family to the airport where we flew to an island in the Caribbean. Adorning all the walls in the hotel were bright signs that read: "Happy Birthday, Lily."

Another quality of Mitch's that others admire is his ability to go-go-go and never stop. I also admire it and can keep up with him most of the time, but sometimes I'd like to just rest and not have to stay so busy. For my birthday, he had made arrangements for us to go parasailing, snorkeling, deep-sea fishing, and sightseeing. It didn't seem right to complain since he'd put so much effort into the whole affair. But after two days, I was exhausted and was just about to say, "Can we go home now?" That's when Mitch threw me the biggest birthday surprise ever.

He said, "Lily, I love you, and I want this to be the best birthday ever. We have three days left, and I want you to tell me what you want to do, anything you want."

"Do you mean it, Mitch?"

"Of course." He grinned. "Absolutely anything."

"All right, then what I really want is to do nothing but enjoy you and our boys. I want to lie on the beach drinking a margarita. I want to take each moment and just be with it. If I feel like doing something, great, if not, then not. I'm tired of having to do so much."

Mitch looked a little surprised, but smiled. "Lily, all you have to do is ask." He gave me what I asked for, and that birthday truly was the best birthday I ever had. I guess those women are right . . . I am the luckiest woman in the world.

FAMOUS DALMATIAN MAN: Jim Carrey as Bruce Nolen in *Bruce Almighty*

There are very few times in the movie where Bruce is still. Most of the time, he's moving faster than the human speed limit. While he wants to please his girlfriend, Grace, he's too caught up in his experiences to see what she wants. He brings her exotic flowers he created and pulls the moon closer to earth trying to make her happy, not recognizing that what she really wants is his attention on her and a proposal of marriage.

QUALITIES:

- EAGER TO PLEASE BUT SLIGHTLY INDEPENDENT
- EXTREMELY INTELLIGENT
- MULTITALENTED
- VERY BALANCED

FINE FOR NOVICE WOMEN

Behavior with children:		🦴🦴🦴
Exercise required:		🦴🦴
Activity level:	🦴🦴 or	🦴🦴🦴
Ease of training:		🦴🦴🦴
Sociability with strangers:		🦴🦴
Affection level:		🦴🦴🦴
Playfulness:		🦴🦴🦴
Protectiveness:	🦴🦴 or	🦴🦴🦴
Watchdog ability:		🦴🦴🦴

PHYSICAL CHARACTERISTICS: Poodle men come in all sizes: very small, medium, and large. They usually have curly hair, and you'll see some interesting haircuts on Poodle men who like to show off their lovely locks. Some men prefer their hair long and tend to be a bit flamboyant, while others keep it trimmed short, wearing a sporty look. Poodle men tend to have athletic physiques.

ABILITIES & INTERESTS: Poodle men are witty, fun-loving, and intelligent. Some sources say they are the most intelligent breed of men. They make excellent "idea" men in a corporate setting such as advertising. They have a strong desire to please and will respond well to instructions from others, but they can also think for themselves. Poodle men are also natural performers, so you'll find them in the circus, Hollywood, comedy clubs, or the theater. Although the standard Poodle man is fun-loving, he's quite serious about his work and therefore takes pride in a job well done. He can easily spend hours absorbed in a project, and then when he has free time, relax and enjoy himself. Poodle men are very athletic and enjoy sports, whether in groups or by themselves.

TRAINING: A Poodle man is easy to train because he is so intelligent and wants to please others. Never treat a Poodle man as if he's stupid. You'll only humiliate him and hurt his feelings if you do. Because a Poodle man likes to please others, when you ask him to do something, chances are it's done. Be careful not to spoil a Poodle man, especially the smaller ones. Some women want to lavish him with love and attention and turn him into a pampered "plaything." Keep in mind that the more you spoil him, the more demanding he may become.

SOCIAL SKILLS: Poodles respond well to strangers most of the time. They may take their time getting to know someone but generally they're trusting. If they don't trust someone, chances are you shouldn't either. Poodle men enjoy the company of others and usually have a wide variety of friends; that way whatever mood they are in, they will have a friend to meet that mood. Due to their even temper and loving nature, Poodle men can make excellent family men. With children they can be playful, loving, devoted, and, if necessary, the disciplinarian. In a relationship, these men are very affectionate and playful but not too demanding. They like their space but are comfortable sharing it.

TYPE OF WOMAN: The best woman for a Poodle man is fun-loving, playful, and intelligent. She can be serious but knows how to let her hair down. She will enjoy his public displays and showy antics. His desire to please her and his attentiveness will please her immensely, and she will know better than to take him for granted.

TYPICAL POODLE MAN: Jon's story, as told by his fiancée, Cindy:

What was I doing wrong? Why did every relationship begin, continue, and end in frustration, heartache, and suffering? Was there something wrong with me? Were all guys impossible for me? I was ready to give up about the time I went to visit Jeannette. She told me about her book and, apparently, I had been dating a Doberman, a Pit Bull, and a German Shepherd. All good breeds for the right woman, but the breed Jeannette said would suit me best was a Poodle. I had been barking up the wrong trees.

About five months after my visit with Jeannette, I moved to Maui. While surfing one afternoon, I met Jon. I thought he was handsome, kind, and quiet. At the time I was not interested in dating or having a relationship because I was focused on starting my practice and was completely intolerant of any hassles that could potentially come from having a relationship with a man . . . even if he was a Poodle! But as time went on and I went surfing with my friends, from time to time I would find myself floating in the water next to Jon while waiting for waves. He was always very pleasant to be around and fun to be with. We became friends and when the time came to work hard to get my office open, Jon offered to help. I had intended to do everything myself, but because I didn't feel intimidated by Jon and I enjoyed his company, I decided to accept his offer.

Having Jon to help turned out to be a true blessing as I had completely underestimated the amount of work that needed to be done. There was so much to do and Jon genuinely enjoyed doing it. Many times Jon would do things before I could even think of what needed to be done. At the same time, he wasn't obnoxiously in my face. He gave me space. He was extremely intelligent and great at problem solving. It was so easy and enjoyable to spend time with Jon. And the more I got to know him, the more time I wanted to spend with him.

Jon is also very multitalented. He's the one you would want to come running if you're lying unconscious with your head gashed open. Jon can also repair just about everything from crashing computers to exploding hot water heaters, prepare delicious meals, and do major construction work. He also finds time to surf and play golf. Surprisingly, while Jon is definitely a man with a shy and serene disposition, he can also be quite the showman. He has everyone on the beach cheering when he hangs ten!

I am amazed by how easy our relationship has been. There is no drama, no heartaches, no hassles, not even any quarrels! I am amazed by how fun, loving, intimate, and rewarding our time together is. When Jeannette came to visit last winter, she confirmed, "Jon is a Poodle." Yes, I thought, I finally picked the right breed! Jon, however, was not thrilled about being a Poodle until he found out that many women would love to be in a relationship with a Poodle man. He's a "hot commodity." He also liked knowing Poodles are the most intelligent of all breeds. Comfortable in his masculinity, Jon is now proud to be my Poodle!

FAMOUS POODLE MAN: Jerry Seinfeld on *Seinfeld*

Jerry's extremely creative and intelligent. As a standup comedian who finds humor in life, others, and himself, he knows how to combine work with play. Jerry loves attention, but he doesn't draw attention with his looks. Instead, he uses his clever observations and dialogue to draw an audience. He's eager to please others, but he's not the kind of guy who will fawn all over someone in an attempt to make her happy.

Conclusion
WOMAN'S BEST FRIEND

As I write this conclusion, my Borzoi dog, Strider, walked over and licked my face. I feel blessed to have him in my life. I also feel blessed to have Lance, my Borzoi man, by my side. If someone had told me years ago that my love relationship would be this easy, this fun, and this fulfilling, I would have questioned his sanity. Based on previous experience, that had not been my life. Past relationships had been a struggle for me, in part because I never felt comfortable enough to be myself. I realize now it wasn't just the past men in my life who were the problem. The problem was also my inability to be in a relationship with them. I knew they wouldn't change so I tried to be different, to fit them. And while they may have thought the relationship was easy for them, it wasn't for me.

Lance has challenging aspects, and his ex-girlfriends and ex-wife could tell you stories that

"He is your friend, your partner, your defender, your dog. You are his life, his love, his leader. He will be yours, faithful and true, to the last beat of his heart. You owe it to him to be worthy of such devotion."
UNKNOWN

may make you wonder how any woman could be happy with him. But for me, he's easy. I understand and appreciate him just the way he is. I have no desire to change him. Twelve years we've been together, and I still wonder at how much I love and respect him. I believe that if I can have a relationship filled with so much love and understanding, it's possible for all women. It's a matter of finding the man most suitable for a particular woman.

If you date a guy and love him, but you realize there are things you want to be different, even one thing, then I encourage you to think seriously before continuing the relationship or marrying him. If I ask you, "Could you live the rest of your life with this man if these characteristics never change?" and you say "No," then I would say, "What are you thinking?" You may believe you'll never find someone better. Or you may be in a situation concerned about bigger matters such as your children's needs or your financial situation. Even then, *would you be willing to live the rest of your life with a man whose nature will continue to challenge you and maybe even make you miserable?*

Is this the relationship that you choose for yourself?

Knowing what I know now, I'd rather be alone than be with the wrong man for the wrong reasons. Would you be willing to wait until you're 30, 40, 50, maybe even 60 or older, to find the right man? There are some things worth waiting for, like a beautiful sunset, finding just the right home to live in, and a baby to be born. I would add a good man to the list. I would encourage you to believe in yourself, to believe that you can have everything you desire in a man.

If you decide, for whatever reason, to marry a man who has something about him that causes you concern, or if you are already married to a man who challenges you, then I encourage you to have compassion for him and yourself. Find ways to love him for his positive attributes, for those qualities you admire. If it helps, think of him as the dog breed he matches. A friend of mine married an Akita who was very possessive. Every time he became jealous, she pictured an Akita dog and how she would reassure the dog that she was okay, that she appreciated his willingness to protect her, that he could relax and let it go. This mind-set helped her to communicate with her husband in such a way that he would ease up rather than become more jealous and possessive.

We all want to be loved and appreciated for who we are. It would be wonderful if simultaneously, in a relationship, men and women could always love and respect one another, but this is not always the case, especially when events have created tension in the relationship. I encourage you to focus on the good in your man, learn to treat him with respect if you don't already. Often, when a woman takes steps to honor him, he'll eventually return it to her. Depending on how long the tension has gone on or how deep the emotional challenges are, he may test her and be even more difficult. You would think we would welcome change, especially loving changes, but often people try to hold on to the old patterns, even when they cause disharmony. But if a woman is persistent in her behavior and continues to show love, compassion, and acceptance, most men will at some point come around and respond in kind. I'm not telling women to be doormats for a man to walk all over. I'm asking women to be clear about the way they treat a man. Treat him the way you would want to be treated, show him the respect you would like to receive, and, even more important, treat him the way you know he wants to be treated. If you like gifts but you know he'd prefer a few nice words of praise and a quiet evening, then give him that.

The biggest present you can give a man is letting him be who he is and letting him have his experiences. Sometimes we take things personally that aren't personal. Sometimes men try to make it personal, but we know it's not. To give another the freedom to go through whatever they're going through is a message of love. It says, "I love you, regardless." By honoring his experience or process, you don't have to take it on or be around it necessarily, but you can send the message out that it's okay and you will continue to love him.

My friend Rick is a prime example. Rick travels on occasion. Before every trip he becomes irritable and his wife, Carla, knows to expect certain behavior from him. Although she doesn't like the behavior, she knows he'll be more loving when he returns so she lets it go. One day she had to go out of town to take care of her aunt, and Carla realized she, too, was irritable. She was also surprised to notice that she directed it at Rick. He knew what she was going through and lovingly allowed her the freedom to feel her frustration, as she allowed him.

My wish for men and women is that they find that special person who brings greater meaning to their lives and that they live together happily. For every woman who has already found the breed of man who matches her values, needs, and desires . . . congratulations! My hope is that this book helps you understand him deeper so that you can strengthen your relationship with him.

For those women still searching, may you find the man who allows you to be who you are. A man you can love for who he is. For every woman, there is a right breed of man. A perfect match. Be willing to wait until you find him. He's out there searching for the right woman for him. Always believe that you deserve a healthy, happy relationship full of love and harmony. Focus on the relationship you want and create that.

Charts

Airedale Terrier

Akita

American Cocker
    Spaniel

American Pit Bull

Australian Shepherd

Basset Hound

Beagle

Bloodhound

Borzoi

Boxer

Brittany

Bulldog

Bull Terrier

Chihuahua

Chow Chow

Collie

Dachshund

Dalmatian

Doberman Pinscher

German Shepherd

Golden Retriever

Great Dane

Irish Setter

Labrador Retriever

Maltese

Mastiff

Miniature Schnauzer

Norwegian Elkhound

Old English Sheepdog

Parson (Jack) Russell
    Terrier

Pekingese

Poodle

Pug

Rhodesian Ridgeback

Rottweiler

Saint Bernard

Schnauzer

Scottish Terrier

Shih Tzu

Siberian Husky

Weimaraner

West Highland White
    Terrier

CHART 1

Breed	Women	Children	Exercise	Activity	Training	Sociability
Airedale Terrier	Experienced	Moderate	Moderate	Moderate	Moderate	High
Akita	Experienced	Low	Moderate	Low	Moderate	Low
American Cocker Spaniel	Novice	High	Moderate	Moderate	High	High
American Pit Bull	Experienced	Low	Moderate	High	Low	Moderate
Australian Shepherd	Experienced	High	Moderate	Moderate	High/Moderate	Moderate
Basset Hound	Novice	High	Moderate	Low	Moderate	Moderate
Beagle	Novice	High	Moderate	High	Moderate	High
Bloodhound	Experienced	High	High	Low	Low	High
Borzoi	Experienced	Moderate	Moderate	Low	Low	Moderate
Boxer	Novice	High	Moderate	Moderate	Low	Moderate
Brittany	Novice	High	High	Moderate	High	Moderate
Bulldog	Novice	High	Low	Low	Moderate	Moderate
Bull Terrier	Experienced	Moderate	Moderate	Moderate	Low	Low
Chihuahua	Novice	Moderate	Low	High	Moderate/Low	Low
Chow Chow	Experienced	Moderate	Moderate	Low	Low	Low
Collie	Novice	Moderate	Moderate	Low	Moderate	Moderate
Dachshund	Novice	Moderate	Low	High	Moderate	Low
Dalmatian	Experienced	High	High	High	Moderate	Moderate
Doberman Pinscher	Experienced	Low	Moderate	High/Moderate	High/Moderate	Low
German Shepherd	Experienced	High	Moderate	Moderate	High/Moderate	Low
Golden Retriever	Novice	High	Moderate	Moderate	High	High
Great Dane	Novice	High	Moderate	Moderate	Moderate	Moderate
Irish Setter	Novice	High	High	High	High/Moderate	High
Labrador Retriever	Novice	High	Moderate	Moderate	High	High
Maltese	Novice	Moderate	Low	High	Moderate	Moderate
Mastiff	Experienced	High	Moderate	Low	Moderate	Moderate
Miniature Schnauzer	Novice	Moderate	Moderate	High/Moderate	Moderate	Moderate
Norwegian Elkhound	Experienced	Moderate	Moderate	Moderate	Low	Moderate
Old English Sheepdog	Experienced	High	Moderate	Moderate	Low	Moderate
Parson Russell Terrier	Novice	Moderate	Moderate	High	Moderate	Moderate
Pekingese	Novice	Moderate	Low	Low	Low	Low
Poodle	Novice	High	Moderate	High/Moderate	High	Moderate
Pug	Novice	High	Low	Low	Moderate	Moderate
Rhodesian Ridgeback	Experienced	Moderate	High	Low	Low	Low
Rottweiler	Experienced	Low	Moderate	Low	Moderate	Low
Saint Bernard	Experienced	High	Moderate	Low	Low	Moderate
Schnauzer	Experienced	Moderate	Moderate	Moderate	Moderate	Low
Scottish Terrier	Novice	Moderate	Moderate	Moderate	Low	Low
Shih Tzu	Novice	Moderate	Low	Moderate	Moderate	Moderate
Siberian Husky	Experienced	High	Moderate	High	Low	High
Weimaraner	Experienced	Moderate	High	High	Low	Moderate
West Highland White Terrier	Novice	Moderate	Moderate	High	Moderate	High

For use in answering the questions in the previous chapters 2 and 3 and choosing your breed of man, see example 1. Feel free to copy and cut out. Then you can place one of these across chart 1 and slide it down the list of breeds to find the most appropriate breed match.

EXAMPLE 1

BREED	WOMEN	CHILDREN	EXERCISE	ACTIVITY	TRAINING	SOCIABILITY
American Cocker Spaniel	Novice	High	Moderate	Moderate	Hight	High
Golden Retriever						

Fill in answers to Women, Children, Exercise, etc. Then find the breed or breeds.

BREED	WOMEN	CHILDREN	EXERCISE	ACTIVITY	TRAINING	SOCIABILITY

BREED	WOMEN	CHILDREN	EXERCISE	ACTIVITY	TRAINING	SOCIABILITY

CHART 2
NOVICE VERSUS EXPERIENCED WOMEN

FOR NOVICE WOMEN	FOR EXPERIENCED WOMEN
American Cocker Spaniel	Airedale Terrier
Basset Hound	Akita
Beagle	American Pit Bull
Boxer	Australian Shepherd
Brittany	Bloodhound
Bulldog	Borzoi
Chihuahua	Bull Terrier
Collie	Chow Chow
Dachshund	Dalmatian
Golden Retriever	Doberman Pinscher
Great Dane	German Shepherd
Irish Setter	Mastiff
Labrador Retriever	Norwegian Elkhound
Maltese	Old English Sheepdog
Miniature Schnauzer	Rhodesian Ridgeback
Parson Russell Terrier	Rottweiler
Pekingese	Saint Bernard
Poodle	Schnauzer
Pug	Siberian Husky
Scottish Terrier	Weimaraner
Shih Tzu	
West Highland White Terrier	

CHART 3
FOR EXPERIENCED WOMEN DUE TO:

INDEPENDENCE	STUBBORNNESS	AGGRESSIVENESS
Akita	Airedale Terrier	Akita
Australian Shepherd	Akita	American Pit Bull
Bloodhound	American Pit Bull	Chow Chow
Borzoi	Bloodhound	Dalmatian (some)
Bull Terrier	Borzoi	Doberman Pinscher
Norwegian Elkhound	Bull Terrier	German Shepherd
Old English Sheepdog	Chow Chow	Rhodesian Ridgeback
Rhodesian Ridgeback	Dalmatian	Rottweiler
Schnauzer	Mastiff	
Siberian Husky	Norwegian Elkhound	
Weimaraner	Old English Sheepdog	
	Rhodesian Ridgeback	
	Rottweiler	
	Saint Bernard	
	Schnauzer	
	Siberian Husky	
	Weimaraner	

CHART 4
BEHAVIOR WITH CHILDREN

HIGH	MODERATE	LOW
American Cocker Spaniel	Airedale Terrier	Akita
Australian Shepherd	Borzoi	American Pit Bull
Basset Hound	Bull Terrier	Doberman Pinscher
Beagle	Chihuahua	Rottweiler
Bloodhound	Chow Chow	
Boxer	Collie	
Brittany	Dachshund	
Bulldog	Maltese	
Dalmatian	Miniature Schnauzer	
German Shepherd	Norwegian Elkhound	
Golden Retriever	Parson Russell Terrier	
Great Dane	Pekingese	
Irish Setter	Rhodesian Ridgeback	
Labrador Retriever	Schnauzer	
Mastiff	Scottish Terrier	
Old English Sheepdog	Shih Tzu	
Poodle	Weimaraner	
Pug	West Highland White Terrier	
Saint Bernard		
Siberian Husky		

CHART 5
LEVEL OF EXERCISE

HIGH	MODERATE	LOW
Bloodhound	Airedale Terrier	Bulldog
Brittany	Akita	Chihuahua
Dalmatian	American Cocker Spaniel	Dachshund
Irish Setter	American Pit Bull	Maltese
Rhodesian Ridgeback	Australian Shepherd	Pekingese
Weimaraner	Basset Hound	Pug
	Beagle	Shih Tzu
	Borzoi	
	Boxer	
	Bull Terrier	
	Chow Chow	
	Collie	
	Doberman Pinscher	
	German Shepherd	
	Golden Retriever	
	Great Dane	
	Labrador Retriever	
	Mastiff	
	Miniature Schnauzer	
	Norwegian Elkhound	
	Old English Sheepdog	
	Parson Russell Terrier	
	Poodle	
	Rottweiler	
	Saint Bernard	
	Schnauzer	
	Scottish Terrier	
	Siberian Husky	
	West Highland White Terrier	

CHART 6
LEVEL OF ACTIVITY

HIGH	MODERATE	LOW
American Pit Bull	Airedale Terrier	Akita
Beagle	American Cocker Spaniel	Basset Hound
Chihuahua	Australian Shepherd	Bloodhound
Dachshund	Boxer	Borzoi
Dalmatian	Brittany	Bulldog
Doberman Pinscher	Bull Terrier	Chow Chow
Irish Setter	Doberman Pinscher	Collie
Maltese	German Shepherd	Great Dane
Miniature Schnauzer	Golden Retriever	Mastiff
Parson Russell Terrier	Labrador Retriever	Pekingese
Poodle	Miniature Schnauzer	Pug
Siberian Husky	Norwegian Elkhound	Rhodesian Ridgeback
Weimaraner	Old English Sheepdog	Rottweiler
West Highland White Terrier	Poodle	Saint Bernard
	Schnauzer	
	Scottish Terrier	
	Shih Tzu	

CHART 7
EASE OF TRAINING

HIGH	MODERATE	LOW
American Cocker Spaniel	Airedale Terrier	American Pit Bull
Australian Shepherd	Akita	Bloodhound
Brittany	Australian Shepherd	Borzoi
Doberman Pinscher	Basset Hound	Boxer
German Shepherd	Beagle	Bull Terrier
Golden Retriever	Bulldog	Chihuahua
Irish Setter	Chihuahua	Chow Chow
Labrador Retriever	Collie	Norwegian Elkhound
Poodle	Dachshund	Old English Sheepdog
	Dalmatian	Parson Russell Terrier
	Doberman Pinscher	Pekingese
	German Shepherd	Rhodesian Ridgeback
	Great Dane	Scottish Terrier
	Irish Setter	Siberian Husky
	Maltese	Weimaraner
	Mastiff	
	Miniature Schnauzer	
	Pug	
	Rottweiler	
	Saint Bernard	
	Schnauzer	
	Shih Tzu	
	West Highland White Terrier	

CHART 8
SOCIABILITY WITH STRANGERS

HIGH	MODERATE	LOW
Airedale Terrier	American Pit Bull	Akita
American Cocker Spaniel	Australian Shepherd	Chihuahua
Beagle	Basset Hound	Chow Chow
Bloodhound	Borzoi	Dachshund
Golden Retriever	Boxer	Doberman Pinscher
Irish Setter	Brittany	German Shepherd
Labrador Retriever	Bulldog	Pekingese
Siberian Husky	Bull Terrier	Rhodesian Ridgeback
West Highland White Terrier	Collie	Rottweiler
	Dalmatian	Schnauzer
	Great Dane	Scottish Terrier
	Maltese	
	Mastiff	
	Miniature Schnauzer	
	Norwegian Elkhound	
	Old English Sheepdog	
	Parson Russell Terrier	
	Poodle	
	Pug	
	Saint Bernard	
	Shih Tzu	
	Weimaraner	

CHART 9
LEVEL OF AFFECTION IN AN INTIMATE RELATIONSHIP

HIGH	MODERATE	LOW
American Cocker Spaniel	Airedale Terrier	Chow Chow
Beagle	Akita	Pekingese
Bloodhound	American Pit Bull	Rottweiler
Boxer	Australian Shepherd	Schnauzer
Brittany	Basset Hound	
Bulldog	Borzoi	
Dalmatian	Bull Terrier	
Golden Retriever	Chihuahua	
Great Dane	Collie	
Irish Setter	Dachshund	
Labrador Retriever	Doberman Pinscher	
Mastiff	German Shepherd	
Miniature Schnauzer	Maltese	
Old English Sheepdog	Norwegian Elkhound	
Poodle	Parson Russell Terrier	
Pug	Rhodesian Ridgeback	
Shih Tzu	Saint Bernard	
Siberian Husky	Scottish Terrier	
West Highland White Terrier	Weimaraner	

CHART 10
LEVEL OF PLAYFULNESS

HIGH	MODERATE	LOW
Airedale Terrier	Akita	Basset Hound
American Cocker Spaniel	American Pit Bull	Bloodhound
Australian Shepherd	Beagle	Chihuahua
Boxer	Borzoi	Chow Chow
Brittany	Bulldog	German Shepherd
Bull Terrier	Collie	Great Dane
Golden Retriever	Dachshund	Mastiff
Irish Setter	Dalmatian	Pekingese
Labrador Retriever	Doberman Pinscher	Rottweiler
Maltese	Norwegian Elkhound	
Miniature Schnauzer	Old English Sheepdog	
Parson Russell Terrier	Pug	
Poodle	Rhodesian Ridgeback	
Shih Tzu	Saint Bernard	
Siberian Husky	Schnauzer	
Weimaraner	Scottish Terrier	
	West Highland White Terrier	

CHART 11
LEVEL OF PROTECTIVENESS

HIGH	MODERATE	LOW
Airedale Terrier	Australian Shepherd	American Cocker Spaniel
Akita	Borzoi	Basset Hound
American Pit Bull	Boxer	Beagle
Chow Chow	Bull Terrier	Bloodhound
Doberman Pinscher	Collie	Brittany
German Shepherd	Dalmatian	Bulldog
Mastiff	Great Dane	Chihuahua
Norwegian Elkhound	Old English Sheepdog	Dachshund
Rhodesian Ridgeback	Poodle	Golden Retriever
Rottweiler		Irish Setter
Schnauzer		Labrador Retriever
Weimaraner		Maltese
		Miniature Schnauzer
		Parson Russell Terrier
		Pekingese
		Poodle (Miniature)
		Pug
		Saint Bernard
		Scottish Terrier
		Shih Tzu
		Siberian Husky
		West Highland White Terrier

CHART 12
LEVEL OF WATCHDOG ABILITY

HIGH	MODERATE	LOW
Airedale Terrier	American Cocker Spaniel	Bulldog
Akita	Basset Hound	Saint Bernard
American Pit Bull	Beagle	
Australian Shepherd	Bloodhound	
Bull Terrier	Borzoi	
Chihuahua	Boxer	
Chow Chow	Brittany	
Collie	Dalmatian	
Dachshund	Golden Retriever	
Doberman Pinscher	Great Dane	
German Shepherd	Irish Setter	
Maltese	Labrador Retriever	
Mastiff	Old English Sheepdog	
Miniature Schnauzer	Shih Tzu	
Norwegian Elkhound	Siberian Husky	
Parson Russell Terrier	West Highland White Terrier	
Pekingese		
Poodle		
Pug		
Rhodesian Ridgeback		
Rottweiler		
Schnauzer		
Scottish Terrier		
Weimaraner		

ABOUT THE AUTHOR

Photo by John Pingenot

JEANNETTE WRIGHT

Jeannette lives with her husband, Lance, and their canine and feline companions in Texas.

ABOUT THE ILLUSTRATOR

MIKE MCCARTNEY

For the past 25 years, Mike McCartney has been a commercial artist living in Door County, Wisconsin: a peninsula on Lake Michigan.

McCartney started out his career by setting up his easel and drawing caricatures of people at local art shows. He then worked his way into the commercial art world specializing in whimsical art. In 1991 at a Great Dane National Specialty, McCartney started creating caricatures ringside, and word spread quickly about his style of capturing a dog's personality in any situation. What an overwhelming response! McCartney's ideas were flowing with ease and fun. It was then and there, McCartney decided to focus on the pet world with his own playful view.

His collection features 150 different breeds and thousands of designs, with several unique styles of illustrations. His artwork can be found on note cards, shirts, mugs, calendars, etc. He promises to continuously add new artwork as a result of all the input received from animal lovers across the country.

His wife, Diana, and children, Butch and Stevi, all work together in their family operation. You can visit his Web site at www.mccartneysdogs.com.